W9-BMT-399

CULTURES OF THE WORLD
Iceland

Cavendish
Square
New York

Published in 2017 by Cavendish Square Publishing, LLC
243 5th Avenue, Suite 136, New York, NY 10016
Copyright © 2017 by Cavendish Square Publishing, LLC

Third Edition

Library of Congress Cataloging-in-Publication Data

Names: Wilcox, Jonathan, 1960- author. | Latif, Zawiah Abdul, co-author. | Nevins, Debbie, co-author.
Title: Iceland / Jonathan Wilcox, Zawiah Abdul Latif, and Debbie Nevins.
Description: Third edition. | New York : Cavendish Square Publishing, [2017] | Series: Cultures of the world |
Includes bibliographical references and index.
Identifiers: LCCN 2016040410 (print) | LCCN 2016041036 (ebook) | ISBN 9781502622181 (library bound) | ISBN 9781502622211 (E-book)
Subjects: LCSH: Iceland--Juvenile literature.
Classification: LCC DL305 .W55 2017 (print) | LCC DL305 (ebook) | DDC 949.12--dc23
LC record available at https://lccn.loc.gov/2016040410

Writers, Jonathan Wilcox and Zawiah Abdul Latif; Debbie Nevins, third edition
Editorial Director, third edition: David McNamara
Editor, third edition: Debbie Nevins
Associate Art Director, third edition: Amy Greenan
Designer, third edition: Jessica Nevins
Production Coordinator, third edition: Karol Szymczuk
Cover Picture Researcher: Angela Siegel
Picture Researcher, third edition: Jessica Nevins

PRECEDING PAGE
The Strokkur Geyser erupts at the Haukadalur geothermal area in Iceland.

CONTENTS

ICELAND TODAY

ICELAND MIGHT JUST AS EASILY HAVE BEEN NAMED SNOWLAND, Greenland, Glacierland, or Volcanoland—any of those names would have been just as fitting. This isolated island in the North Atlantic Ocean is often called the "land of fire and ice." One-third of the country is covered by ice, yet volcanic activity creates an abundance of natural hot springs and geysers. This dramatic landscape makes the island uninhabitable across much of its interior, so most of the people live on its periphery, which can be quite green, at least in the summertime.

Other names for the country—at least in recent years—could be Peaceland or Happyland. In 2016, the Institute for Economics and Peace ranked Iceland number one out of 162 countries on its Global Peace Index for the sixth year in a row. In fact, Iceland has held the top spot on that index every year since the list was begun in 2008, except for 2010, when it came in at number two. This evaluation measures a country's relative peacefulness based on such indicators as its active wars and conflicts, political instability, terrorist activity, violent crime, imprisoned population, and weapons capabilities. In those categories and others like them, Iceland scores "none" or "nearly none."

Peace and happiness go hand-in-hand, so it's not surprising to find that in a separate ranking—the 2016 World Happiness Report—Iceland was number three out of 157 countries. In this report, indicators contributing to a country's "gross national happiness" include social support, freedom to make life choices, healthy life expectancy, generosity, trust in government and business, and the gross domestic product (GDP) per capita. (GDP is an economic measurement of a nation's total economic activity, the monetary value of all its goods and services produced over a certain period of time. Typically, a higher GDP number indicates a healthier economy.)

If any country has earned the right to chant "We're Number One," it's Iceland. In 2013, the World Economic Forum (WEF) found Icelanders to be the world's friendliest people in their attitude toward foreign visitors. In 2016, the WEF rated Iceland first in the world for gender equality. In 2012, the country was number one for safety and security (falling only to number two in subsequent years), said the Legatum Prosperity Index. There are many such ratings indexes, all measuring the world's countries according to somewhat different criteria. Such reports attempt to quantify the elusive characteristics that define a good life, and determine which country offers its people the best chance at living that life.

Iceland typically does well in these rankings, though it's not the richest country on earth. In some ways, the island's success is a paradox. From a climatic perspective, it's hardly a tropical paradise. In July, the average temperature in the southern part of the island is a sweater-weather 50—55 degrees Fahrenheit (10—13 degrees Celsius), though summer days can occasionally reach into the mid-70s°F (mid-20s°C). The warm season is short, and the cold season is not only long, but dark. In Reykjavik, the capital city located in the southwest of the island, the December sun barely peeks above the horizon for about four hours a day.

Long, cold, dark days would seem like indicators for high rates of depression, not happiness. Curiously, Iceland tops out in the blue-mood category as well. In a well-publicized 2013 report by the Organization for Economic Cooperation and Development (OECD), Icelanders ranked number one out of twenty-five countries for antidepressant use. These results

Tourists stand on icebergs in the glacial Lake Jokulsarlon in southeast Iceland.

A woman enjoys Iceland's most popular hot spring, the Blue Lagoon.

beg the question: Are Icelanders the world's happiest people despite their antidepressant use, or because of it? The answer, if there even is one, is unclear. Some analysts caution against assuming any sort of correlation between the two statistics, but the paradox is intriguing.

In terms of social mores, Iceland again turns the traditional status quo upside down. The marriage rate is declining, while the rate of children born outside of marriage is on the rise. In 2016, the country led the world in that category—more than two-thirds, or 67 percent, of Icelandic babies were born out of wedlock. This is a trend in the Nordic countries as a group, and is not commonly seen as a problem there. In fact, for a country that was founded by the reputedly ultramasculine Vikings—as Iceland was more than 1,145 years ago—it is now one of the most feminist countries on earth. In 1980, Iceland became the first country to elect a female president.

Icelanders are great readers. The literacy rate is nearly 100 percent, and the small country publishes more books per capita than anywhere else. In fact, books are such popular gifts at Christmastime that people have a word for the tradition—*Jolabokaflod*, or the "Christmas book flood." Icelanders traditionally give gifts on Christmas Eve, and then spend the holiday night reading. With all those readers, it figures that Iceland also has the world's highest percentage of writers. In 2011, Reykjavik was named by the United Nations Educational, Scientific and Cultural Organization (UNESCO) a City of Literature as part of the United Nations (UN)'s Creative Cities Network.

For many reasons, Iceland has become a favorite destination for tourists. For example, Iceland has no mosquitoes. For some people, that could be reason enough to vacation there. Most tourists arrive in the summer for the fair weather and the midnight sun. For three months, the sun hardly sets and the sky remains bright for twenty-four hours. Those who venture to Iceland in the dark winter, however, may be rewarded with nature's own light show, the aurora borealis. Iceland's Thingvellir National Park is said to be one of the best places to see the northern lights.

Tourists also flock to Iceland for the dramatic volcanic scenery, abundant waterfalls and geothermal hot springs, black sand beaches, massive white glaciers, huge whales, adorable puffins, fluffy Icelandic horses, woolly sheep, and of course, the friendly people. So many tourists have descended upon the tiny island nation in recent years that the crowds may prove to be too much of a good thing. The uptick in tourism has certainly been good for the country's economy, but with four times the native population now arriving each year, the island's pristine environment may well suffer.

Iceland is an unusual place, and its 332,000 or so people are well aware of that. Icelanders are proud of their country, and after seven hundred years of foreign rule, they are fiercely independent as well. Their ancestors created the world's first parliamentary democracy, which continues to this day. They put down roots on a craggy, cold, unsettled island—a very long way from anywhere in those days—and founded what today is one of the world's happiest, friendliest, most peaceful, environmentally sound, and economically successful nations.

Lupines bloom on the Stokksnes headland on Iceland's southeastern coast.

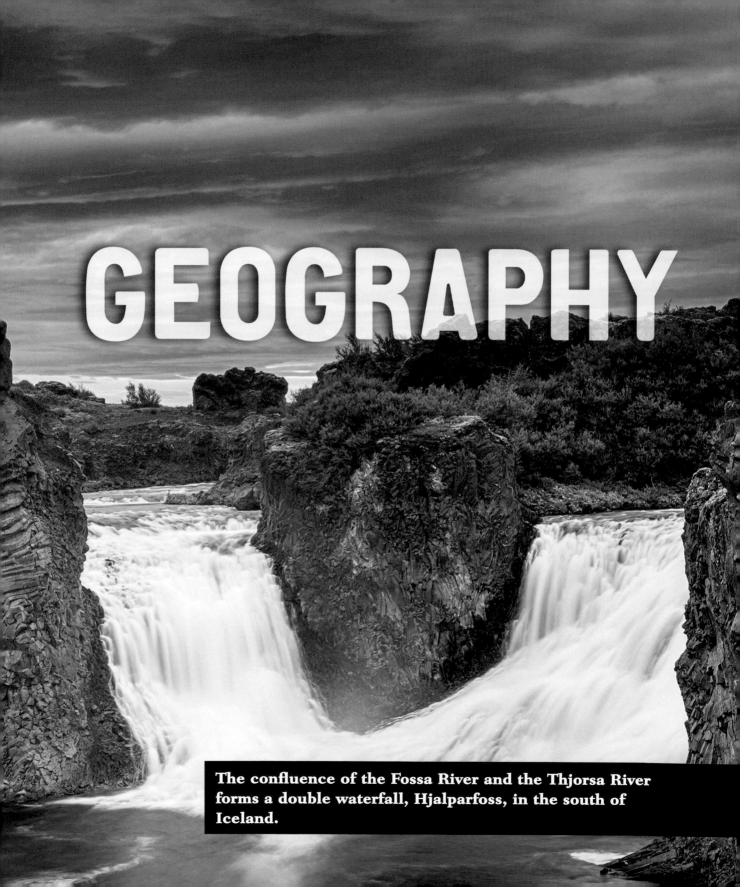

GEOGRAPHY

The confluence of the Fossa River and the Thjorsa River forms a double waterfall, Hjalparfoss, in the south of Iceland.

ICELAND IS OFTEN CALLED THE "LAND of fire and ice." In this case, that is not merely a catchy phrase, but an accurate description. Iceland is, indeed, a land of vast glaciers and active volcanoes. It's also a lively country on an island that straddles the geologic divide between North America and Europe. Historically and culturally, however, it has its roots firmly in Europe.

Iceland sits in the North Atlantic, just south of the Arctic Circle, east of Greenland, and west of the Faroe Islands, which, in turn, lie west of Norway. Iceland is on the same latitude as Fairbanks, Alaska, but is warmed by the flow of the Gulf Stream. The island covers an area that measures approximately 40,000 square miles (103,000 square kilometers), about the size of Ohio.

Much of the island is uninhabitable. Most of the interior is covered by permanent ice or lava, or is a high plateau on which little grows. Human settlement is limited to the rim of the island, where fields have been carved out of the land at the foot of the mountains and where fishing communities have access to the sea. The total population is only about one-third of a million people, about the size of Santa Ana, California.

Mountainous and geologically active with much volcanic activity, Iceland is full of hot springs and rivers, which often flow down spectacular waterfalls on their way to the sea. The harsh terrain and sparse population have left Iceland a country of breathtaking unspoiled natural beauty.

1

Iceland is the second-largest island in Europe, after Great Britain, and the eighteenth-largest island in the world.

REGIONS

The most important division in Iceland is between inhabited and uninhabited land. The uninhabited land is primarily in the interior. Half of this is desert plateau above 1,500 feet (457 meters), where little grows. Eleven percent of the country is covered with glaciers. Iceland's largest glacier, Vatnajokull (Vatna Glacier), is, in volume, the largest ice cap in Europe; in area, it is the second largest, after Austfonna in Norway. It covers 3,100 square miles (8,100 sq km), almost half the area of New Jersey. At some places the ice of this glacier is about 3,300 feet (1,000 m) thick.

Iceland's towns and cities are all located on its outer perimeter because the interior is uninhabitable.

The most important division in Iceland is between inhabited and uninhabited land. The uninhabited land is primarily in the interior. Half of this is desert plateau above 1,500 feet (457 meters), where little grows. Eleven percent of the country is covered with glaciers. Iceland's largest glacier, Vatnajokull (Vatna Glacier), is, in volume, the largest ice cap in Europe; in area, it is the second largest, after Austfonna in Norway. It covers 3,100 square miles (8,100 sq km), almost half the area of New Jersey. At some places the ice of this glacier is about 3,300 feet (1,000 m) thick.

The inhabited part of Iceland is essentially the perimeter of the island. This is served by a single highway that circles the island.

THE SOUTHWEST REGION Over half of the population lives in a small part of the southwest, in and around the capital city of Reykjavik. Extending southwest from Reykjavik is a peninsula of inhospitable lava exposed to the North Atlantic, which is where the international airport is located. Farther south and east of Reykjavik is the best farmland in Iceland. Situated inland is the largest lake, Thingvallavatn, covering 32 square miles (83 sq km). On its shore is Thingvellir, the site of the first Icelandic parliament. Also found here are the geysers at Geysir.

THE SOUTH Off the south coast are the Westmann Islands, harsh volcanic islands that include Surtsey, newly formed by a volcanic eruption in 1963.

On the mainland in the southeast, the glacier Vatnajokull extends almost to the sea. Along the southern coast are numerous *sandur* (SAND-or), wastelands of black sand and volcanic debris deposited by the glacial runoffs, along with innumerable rivers.

THE NORTH Iceland's second-largest city, Akureyri, is at the head of a fjord in the north center of the island. East of it is Myvatn, also known as Midge Lake, in a fertile valley close to fields of lava. Grimsey, a small island off the north coast, is the only part of Iceland to extend into the Arctic Circle.

A road passes through Vatnajokull National Park.

THE WESTERN FJORDS The northwest is marked by deep fjords and steep mountains and is inhabited almost wholly by fishing communities. One entire peninsula, Hornstrandir, has experienced depopulation since the first half of the twentieth century. Since the area is rich in bird life nesting on the cliffs, it has been designated a nature reserve.

CLIMATE

The climate of Iceland is moderate. The warming effect of the Gulf Stream keeps temperatures in Reykjavik from falling much below freezing. The average January temperature in Reykjavik is 31°F (-0.6°C). Iceland's position in the northern North Atlantic prevents summers from getting hot. The average July temperature in Reykjavik is 52°F (11.2°C).

Reykjavik is exposed to the prevailing southwesterly winds blowing in from the Atlantic and as a result is subject to considerable rain. It averages three clear days in January, and only one entirely clear day in July! Rain and cloud cover are less relentless in other parts of Iceland. In the north and east the average summer temperature is warmer than Reykjavik, but winter temperatures are cooler.

"There was a man named Flóki Vilgerdarson, who was a great Viking." So begins the story that explains the naming of the island as recounted in Landnámabók *("The Book of Settlements"), the medieval account of the first settlers. Sometime around the year 870, Flóki set out from Norway with his companions, intending to settle on the newly discovered island.*

The island was then known as Gardarshólmi, after the Swedish Viking Gardar Svavarsson. He was the first to circumnavigate the island, sometime in the 860s, thus establishing that the landmass was, in fact, an island. Gardar spent a winter there, and named the entire place after himself. Another early visitor, the Viking Naddod, also discovered and named the island around the same time. He called it Snaeland, *meaning "Snowland."*

According to the story, Flóki and the other settlers brought livestock with them to the island. They stayed for the summer in the western fjords and enjoyed the good fishing and seal-catching, but made no preparations to support their livestock through the winter. As a result, when winter came and snow covered the land, the animals died from lack of hay. In early spring, Flóki climbed a mountain to assess their prospects and looked out over a fjord full of ice. Discouraged, he named the place Ísland, *meaning "ice land," and returned, after further misadventures, to Norway, where he spoke ill of the new country to discourage people from going there.*

Curiously, a similar ancient tale from the same time period credits the Viking Erik the Red with naming Greenland "green" in an effort to attract Norwegians to settle there. In truth, of course, Greenland is mostly covered in ice, and Iceland is quite green in the summer.

Even more curious, perhaps, is a modern theory that the name "Ísland" has nothing to do with ice. Irish monks lived on the island for centuries before the arrival of the Norse settlers, and these solitary religious men might well have named the land after Jesus, who, in Old Gaelic is called Ísu—hence, Ísuland. Possible? Maybe, but no one knows for sure.

In the northwest, snow falls on an average of one hundred days a year, while the southeast averages about forty snowy days per year. Strong winds are common throughout Iceland. In the sandur and some areas of the interior, dust storms make travel very difficult. Strong winds frequently close airports throughout Iceland, including the international airport at Keflavík.

LENGTH OF DAYS

Iceland is so far north that the length of the day varies greatly with the time of year. In summer, Iceland is a land of midnight sun; in winter, night never ends.

Strictly speaking, it is only on the northern island of Grímsey that the sun never sets (as seen from sea level) during the summer. Elsewhere in Iceland, only a brief period of twilight marks nights in June and July. Icelanders take full advantage of this period. Even little children tend to stay up late in the summer, when outdoor activities of all kinds are at a peak.

Conversely, in mid-winter daylight is limited to a few hours of twilight in the middle of the day. In the communities surrounded by steep fjords,

The midnight sun shines on the town of Grundarfjordur in northwest Iceland.

An Icelandic arctic fox protects her cubs.

particularly in the western fjords, the sight of the sun may be blocked throughout the winter until February or March. Icelanders tend to sleep more during the winter and many suffer from "short-day depression." The first sighting of the sun in the western fjords is greeted by a festival.

FLORA

When the first settlers arrived, about 25 percent of the island was covered in birch forests. Deforestation occurred so quickly that early Icelanders had to search for timber elsewhere, which led to the Viking discovery of North America. Soil erosion accompanied deforestation and was further aggravated by sheep grazing. Today, about a quarter of the country is covered by a continuous carpet of vegetation.

Mosses and lichens are the first plant life to appear on new lava fields. Nearly 500 types of moss and 450 types of lichen grow in Iceland. Marshes and bogs along the coastal wetlands support the growth of grasses and rushes. Blueberry and crowberry bushes grow on the heaths.

FAUNA

The only land mammal native to Iceland that predates human settlement is the arctic fox. Polar bears are rare visitors to Iceland; these animals occasionally drift across on pack ice from Greenland. A variety of rodents, including the rat and the mouse, were accidentally introduced into Iceland by settlers. Reindeer were introduced from Norway in the eighteenth century and now roam wild in the east of the country.

In the sea, marine mammals are more numerous and diverse. Seals are common; both harbor seals and gray seals breed on the coasts. Walruses are rare. Whales were once common, but overhunting has made them less so. The killer whale, or orca, is now the most common, and there are occasional sightings of sperm, fin, humpback, and minke whales. More than three hundred species of fish are found in Iceland's waters.

Iceland is a bird-watcher's paradise. About 85 species breed here, while another 330 species have been spotted. Inland birds include the gyrfalcon, a large falcon found only in Iceland; the white-tailed eagle, a bird of prey related to the American bald eagle; and the ptarmigan, a species of grouse hunted by both gyrfalcons and humans. There are many species of ducks, including eider, the sea-based duck whose feathers are valued for their warmth and softness in the making of eiderdown. Above

Five puffins stand on a rock.

all, there are vast colonies of sea birds, including gannets, fulmars, kittwakes, guillemots, and many more.

Three species of bird deserve special mention. The great auk was a large, flightless seabird that is now extinct. The last recorded specimen was killed in Iceland in 1844.

Puffins are Iceland's most common birds, with a population of eight to ten million. The Westmann Islands off the country's southwestern coast are particularly important nesting grounds for these birds. Puffins catch fish at sea and make nests by digging burrows into sea cliffs in huge communities. However, they are considered a delicacy by Icelanders and are hunted for food by puffin-catchers.

Arctic terns also nest extensively throughout Iceland. These birds migrate each winter from Antarctica, 10,000 miles (16,093 km) away. If animals or people get too close to their nesting colonies, these birds protect their eggs and young by dive-bombing intruders, screeching the sound *kría*, which is their name in Icelandic.

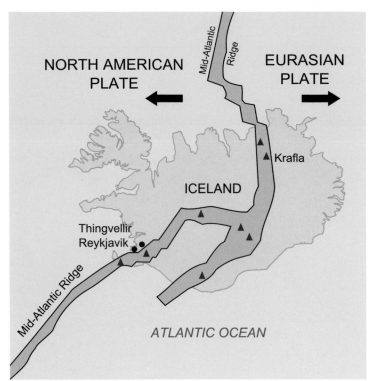

VOLCANIC ACTIVITY

Iceland is situated at the point where two tectonic plates meet. These are vast land masses that float on the earth's central magma. The plate supporting North America is pulling away from the plate supporting Europe and Africa. The movement of the plates results in earthquakes and volcanic eruptions. The gap is filled with lava. As a result, Iceland is growing by up to 1 inch (2.5 centimeters) a year.

In the last few centuries, Iceland has experienced an average of one volcanic eruption every five years. The most spectacular eruption in the twentieth century took place in the Westmann Islands. Between November 1963 and June 1967, a volcano erupted on the sea bottom. This gave birth to a new island, Surtsey, made of lava pushed up from under the sea. Life-forms are slowly becoming established on this island, giving scientists a rare opportunity to study the creation of new land and the growth of new life. Only researchers are allowed on the island.

An eruption in the same area occurred on the island of Heimaey in 1973. A volcano exploded without warning, threatening to cover Heimaey in lava and ash. The entire population was evacuated to safety on boats.

The volcano continued to pour forth lava for five months, sending out 33 million tons (30 million metric tons) of debris. The flow threatened to block the island's harbor. In an attempt to forestall this, at the suggestion of a physicist named Thorbjörn Sigurgeirsson, cold sea water was sprayed onto the 500-foot- (150 m) high wall of lava, which was advancing at 100 feet (30 m) per day. This may have helped to stop the flow. The wall of lava eventually halted 500 feet (150 m) short of blocking the harbor entrance. A third of the town was buried under the lava, while the size of the island

Deep under Iceland's surface, the massive North American tectonic plate meets the Eurasian tectonic plate. This is essentially where the two continents collide, causing great geologic activity that generates Iceland's volcanoes and earthquakes.

expanded by 15 percent. Instead of blocking the harbor, the lava created a more sheltered entrance.

The volcano Bardarbunga erupts in 2014.

In March 2010, a volcanic eruption on the Eyjafjalla Glacier continued on and off for weeks. Although it was not a large eruption, its ash cloud caused a tremendous disruption to air travel across western and northern Europe for several days. During a six-day travel ban, more than ninety-five thousand flights were canceled. An eruption in May 2011 of the Grimsvotn volcano in the southeast Highlands region also disrupted air travel, though to a lesser degree. More recently, from 2014 to 2015, the Bardarbunga volcano in the Highlands region erupted but caused no problem to air traffic.

Geological activity is evident in other features besides the eruption of volcanoes. Near the volcanoes are areas of hot ground, known as *solfataras*, where vents emit hot gases or vapors. Underground heat results in hot springs. At places, when enough pressure builds, these hot springs spout forth jets of hot water. Great Geysir used to spout regularly to a height of 200 feet (60 m) but is now largely inactive, although earthquakes in the area

Snowcapped mountains rise behind Iceland's capital city, Reykjavik.

occasionally revive it. It is often a surprise when it suddenly erupts, such as it did recently in February 2016. Other geysers in the same area still spout, however, including Strokkur, which erupts every few minutes, spewing out hot water to a height of up to 100 feet (30 m).

The energy contained in geological hot spots has been extensively harnessed by Icelanders. Hot water is piped to provide heated swimming pools in most Icelandic communities. More advanced technologies are used to heat most buildings with geothermal energy piped in from these hot spots.

CITIES

REYKJAVÍK Reykjavik and its suburbs (with a combined population of 200,850 as of 2012) are home to over half the population of Iceland. It is a clean, modern city, with a harbor and an airport, which handles domestic flights. The international airport is located in Keflavík, south of Reykjavik. Reykjavik is the cultural center of Iceland, boasting a symphony orchestra,

theater, museums, and library, as well as amenities such as hotels and restaurants. It is the site of the university, the parliament, and the major cathedral.

Reykjavik is also the principal commercial and industrial center of Iceland. The region was first settled around 870. In the eighteenth century, a village grew in the area and was granted municipal rights in 1786. Reykjavik became the seat of the Althing (the Icelandic parliament) in 1843. In 1918, Reykjavik was named the capital of Iceland. During World War II, the city was a British and US naval and air base.

Residential homes in Reykjavik are generally built of concrete and sport brightly colored roofs. The city has improved its tourist facilities considerably in the hope that these improved amenities will attract more tourists to Iceland.

AKUREYRI Despite being Iceland's second-largest city, Akureyri is a small town by European standards, with a population of only 18,200 in 2015.

Cruise ships bring tourists to the city of Akureyri on the island's northern coast.

One of the early settlers of Iceland, arriving shortly after Flóki and his companions had given up and left, was Ingólfur Arnarson. Ingólfur set out with his family, Irish slaves, and the trappings of his homestead in Norway, including his high seat, an ornately carved seat that was a sign of status. On reaching the coast of Iceland, he made a vow to Thor that he would settle wherever the pillars supporting his high seat washed ashore, and then cast the pillars into the water.

At first the pillars were not found and Ingólfur spent his first winter on the south coast (at a place now named Ingólfshöfdi). Three years later, his slaves found the pillars in a large bay in the southwest of the country. Ingólfur named the spot Reykjavik, meaning "Smoky Bay," on account of the steam rising from the geothermal springs. Here he built his homestead. Accordingly, Reykjavik is said to have been founded in the year 874, and Ingólfur is honored as "The First Icelander" because he was the first Norseman to remain on the island permanently. (The earlier Irish monks apparently don't count as "Icelanders.")

Reykjavik has retained its name to this day, even though it is probably one of the world's most smoke-free cities, due to its extensive use of clean geothermal power.

This 1850 painting by the Danish painter Johan Peter Raadsig portrays Ingólfur Arnarson commanding that his high seat pillars be erected.

Incorporated as a city in 1786, Akureyri is situated in the middle of the north coast, at the sheltered end of a long fjord. It is a major fishing harbor and also the center for tourism in the northern half of the country.

ÍSAFJÖRDUR   Isafjordur, with a population of 2,777, is the major town on the Vestfirðir (Westfjords) peninsula. A picturesque small town on a harbor, it is located in a valley surrounded by steep mountains. Fishing and fish processing are the city's major economic activities.

A steep wall of rock towers over ships in the harbor at Skutulsfjordur in the Westfjords territory of Iceland.

INTERNET LINKS

guidetoiceland.is
This site has good information and photos, with links to articles about Iceland's mountains, glaciers, and wildlife, with video and audio files.

www.iceland.is/the-big-picture/nature-environment/geography
Information about Iceland's geography, wildlife, volcanoes, and other related topics are found on this site.

reykjavik.is/en
This interesting and comprehensive site is the official site for the city of Reykjavik, in English.

www.sagamuseum.is/overview/ingolfur-arnarson
This museum site tells the story of Ingólfur Arnarson.

www.visiticeland.com
This tourism site has information and photos of Iceland's various regions.

HISTORY

A replica of a Viking settlement on Iceland's southwestern coast near Hofn honors the country's Norse history.

2

UNTIL THE ARRIVAL OF SOME IRISH monks in the eighth century, Iceland was uninhabited. There were no native people living there, and an absence of archaeological evidence suggests there never were. Long after Europe was fully populated, Iceland belonged only to the birds and the arctic foxes.

According to a book written by a monk in 825 CE, a small band of these monks spent summers on Iceland in monastic seclusion from around the year 795 until the Norsemen arrived.

Early Norwegian settlers described seeing such individuals, who carried the accoutrements of their monastic profession in the form of bells and books and who kept away from the Norse settlers. Little else is known of these Irish hermits, except that they left when the pagan (that is, the Norse) settlers began to arrive.

THE SAGA AGE

Much of what is known about the early years of settlement comes from the Icelandic Sagas. These narratives began as detailed oral histories of the events that took place in the ninth, tenth, and early eleventh centuries of Icelandic settlement. They were eventually written down in the thirteenth and fourteenth centuries. Iceland's Saga Age, as it came to be called, lasted from the first year of settlement in 870 CE to about 1056, when the first bishop founded a church at Skálholt. Some

Around 330 BCE, the ancient Greek explorer Pytheas sailed far north "to the end of the world." In his writings, he described a land he called Thule—"six days' sail north of Britain … near the frozen sea" –and mentioned its midnight sun. For centuries, Thule was identified as Iceland or Greenland. Today, new evidence suggests Pytheas was actually in Norway, but Iceland is still sometimes called Thule.

A statue of Ingólfur Arnarson in Reykjavik honors the Norwegian settler of Iceland.

historians extend the Saga Age to the year 1400, when the writing of the sagas abruptly ended for reasons unknown.

SETTLEMENT Around 874 CE, displaced Norwegians started to settle in Iceland. In Norway, King Harald Fairhair was extending his power throughout the country, which led to the exodus of those chieftains who did not want to be subject to the king. Norway also has limited farmland, so there was always need for new land to support a growing population. Other settlers were fleeing quarrels, feuds, or legal action.

These displaced Norwegians raided and settled in England, Scotland, Ireland, parts of France, and the Shetland, Orkney, and Faroe Islands. They either intermarried or made slaves of local people. Since they took their wives and slaves with them to Iceland, the earliest Icelanders were not just of Norwegian stock, but also of Celtic blood. The most notorious slaves among the early settlers were the Irish slaves of Ingólfur Arnarson's brother, Hjörleifur. They rebelled and killed Hjörleifur and his supporters, then fled to remote islands off the south coast of Iceland, where Ingólfur tracked them down and killed them. The islands are now called Vestmanaeyjar (or Westmann Islands), meaning "Islands of the Westmen." "Westmen" was a term Norwegians used to describe the Irish and others "from the west."

Historians estimate that about twenty thousand people moved to Iceland between 874 and 930. By 930, most of Iceland's habitable land had been claimed. Until the end of the tenth century, landholdings were large. Each homestead contained many people and was practically a self-supporting economic unit. Initially, the settlers lived mostly by fishing, but sheep farming soon became the second-most important industry.

ESTABLISHMENT OF THE ALTHING In 930, the first nationwide parliament in Iceland, known as the Althing, was established. Local regional assemblies, called *things*, had already been established for the arbitration of disputes between settler families. Each thing was presided over by a local chieftain. The chieftains founded a national parliament and a high court, collectively known as the Althing, and adopted a general system of laws for the entire country. The Althing became the supreme authority of the land, presided over by a lawspeaker and by the chieftains of the island. It served to arbitrate disputes and to provide a social and commercial focus. It met every year in the summer for two weeks at Thingvellir. The event had something of a carnival air. Goods were traded, stories were recited, and marriages were arranged between families.

A flag marks the location of the first Icelandic Althing in Thingvellir National Park.

Although the idea for the local thing came from Norway, the Althing was unique in medieval Europe because it imposed centralized authority through group consensus rather than through the power of a king. Iceland was exceptional—a medieval nation that lacked a king. The Althing was the first legislative assembly in northern Europe, and one of the world's oldest parliaments.

Legal proceedings were held at the law rock. The chief organizer there was the lawspeaker, who was responsible for reciting from memory one-third of the laws each year, so that all people should know the law, even if they could not read.

At the law rock, cases were presented before judges appointed by chieftains. The judgment process was not entirely just because the complexities of the law often led to a case being decided on technicalities. There was no police force to carry out judgments, so they were enforced by the chieftains. This made it hard to carry out a judgment against those chieftains.

If a judgment was considered unfair, a feud was likely to develop. Medieval Icelanders considered vengeance the most natural form of justice. The support of chieftains was very important for security against such quarrels. There were thirty-six (later thirty-nine) chieftains, known as *godi* (GO-thi), who also acted as pagan priests. People could choose which godi to follow and the power of the godi could be passed on or exchanged.

The other members of society were farmers, their wives, and their families. Women could own property and be considered the head of the household only when widowed. Given the many violent feuds, this often occurred. Children were educated in the household and were put to work on the farm at an early age. Farmers also kept slaves, although slavery gradually died out. Freed slaves became poor laborers who had to support themselves during the harsh winters.

THE ARRIVAL OF CHRISTIANITY The turn of the first millennium brought a great cultural shift as Christianity came to Iceland. Until then, the Icelanders worshipped the Norse gods, including Odin, Thor, Freyr, and Freya. The first Christian missionaries caused disputes and much bloodshed by slandering the heathen gods. But when Norway's King Olaf converted to Christianity, the pressure mounted on the Icelanders to do the same.

In the year 1000, the choice between Christianity and paganism was put in the hands of the lawspeaker, Thorgeir Ljosvetningagodi Thorkelsson, who pondered the issue at the law rock for a day and a night. Thorgeir finally declared that all people should follow one law and that law should be the law of Christianity, although with continuing tolerance for paganism.

DISCOVERIES OF NEW LANDS Icelanders of the Middle Ages were frequent travelers. Many prominent Icelanders journeyed to Norway for trade and adventure, where the sagas depict them as being generally well-received by Norwegian kings. They also traveled to England and continental Europe and discovered new lands to the west. Erik the Red, a Norwegian Viking who lived in Iceland, was exiled from Iceland because of a killing and went west to discover a large ice-covered island, which he named Greenland to entice further settlers. He succeeded in leading Icelanders to settle there around 986 CE and two major settlements remained for several hundred years.

Erik's son, born in Iceland, followed in his father's footsteps. Leif Erikson (ca. 970—ca. 1020) sailed west, intending to explore the North American coast, which had been discovered by chance and bad navigation by a sailor bound for Greenland. Leif sailed the northeast shore of what is now Canada until he was far enough south to find grapes growing. He thus named the land Vínland, meaning "wine-land." He established the first Norse settlement there, at L'Anse aux Meadows in Newfoundland, in what is now Canada.

In 1477, nearly five centuries after Leif discovered Vínland, the young Italian navigator Christopher Columbus visited Iceland. Although he never said as much, it's possible he could have heard stories there of lands to the west (North America), which Icelanders were well aware of. In 1492, Columbus would land in the Bahamas and eventually be credited with "discovering" the Americas.

This old map drawn by Olaus Magnus in the early sixteenth century shows what was known about Iceland (Islandia) at the time.

THE STURLUNGA AGE

The Age of Sagas, the golden era of Icelandic culture, began to go into decline as wealth and power became concentrated among fewer and fewer chieftains. In the thirteenth century, conflicts erupted as some chieftains tried to take over the dominions of others. What followed, beginning around 1220, was a violent time of civil war that lasted about forty-four years. One of the most powerful families of this time was the Sturlungar family.

Snorri Sturluson (1179—1241) was one of the most powerful chieftains. He was also an important poet and saga writer, who wrote *Heimskringla*, a collection of sixteen sagas of the Norwegian kings. He built up his wealth and power through marriage and was a skillful political operator who was twice elected lawspeaker. He helped maintain his own power in Iceland through friendship with the king of Norway, Håkon III.

In 1241 Snorri broke away from King Håkon, who wanted to extend his power over Iceland. Håkon employed a rival chieftain, Gizurr Thorvaldsson,

NATURAL CATASTROPHES

As Iceland suffered political and economic woes after losing its independence, it also endured miseries brought on, at least in part, by the natural world.

THE LITTLE ICE AGE *From about 1300 to about 1850, a period of cooling called the Little Ice Age shifted the climate on the island. Although it wasn't a true ice age, geologically speaking, it did result in a shortening of the growing season, especially in lands near the Arctic Circle. Both Greenland and Iceland, which barely had sufficient crop-growing weather to begin with, experienced shorter growing seasons and colder winters.*

Naturally this brought about severe hardship. In Greenland, all of the Norse settlements became extinct. Iceland did not suffer that fate. However, peasants who could no longer sustain themselves were forced to work for large landowners, and serflike institution developed. The vistarband, *which went into effect around 1490, required that all landless people become farm laborers, bound in servitude to the landowners.*

THE BLACK DEATH *Another kind of calamity arrived in 1402, when a ship arrived from England carrying a deadly disease. The plague epidemic, called the Black Death, had been raging in Europe for decades, and when it finally hit Iceland, it quickly spread through the population. Possibly one-third to one-half of the island's people died, though there are no actual records. In 1494, the plague would return again to Iceland with similar results.*

VOLCANIC ERUPTIONS *From the time of the first settlement, massive floods, landslides, lava flows, poisonous gases, and ash clouds caused by volcanic eruptions regularly killed people and cattle, and destroyed farms. By far the worst eruption disaster took place in 1783. The Laki eruption in southern Iceland continued for eight months, releasing fluoride gases and sulfur dioxide that poisoned the environment and created a haze that spread over Europe, killing thousands there. On Iceland, the Laki eruption killed up to 80 percent of the livestock and proved catastrophic to the human population. A time of great famine followed, reducing the already impoverished population from fifty thousand to thirty-five thousand people. The difficult period following the eruption is known in Iceland as the "Mist Hardships."*

to go after Snorri. Despite the fact that Gizurr had been Snorri's son-in-law, Gizurr pursued Snorri. A large force caught Snorri at home in the middle of the night on September 22, 1241. Snorri tried to escape to a secret hideout built under the kitchen but was betrayed by a servant and assassinated.

After the chaos of the Sturlunga era, Iceland was left in anarchy. The Althing gave King Håkon the right to collect taxes from Icelanders in return for imposing order. Icelandic independence ended in 1264, with the signing of the Old Covenant, and it became a colony of Norway. Thus began a long period of decline for Iceland, which would become one of Europe's poorest nations.

COLONIAL STATUS

Upon the loss of independence, Icelandic godi were replaced by royal officials who enforced the law of the Norwegian king. The king imposed a monopoly on trade and Iceland became dependent on unreliable Norwegian traders.

In 1380, the balance of power shifted among the Scandinavian nations and Norway came under the control of Denmark. Iceland became a colony of Denmark and the trade monopoly was passed to the Danish king, who forbade Iceland to trade with any other country but Denmark. This trade monopoly would last until 1786. Consequently, imported goods had to be bought at the high price imposed by the Danish, who in turn paid low prices for Icelandic fish.

In the middle of the sixteenth century, during the Protestant Reformation, Lutheranism was imposed on Iceland by the Danish king. Lutheranism remains the official religion of Iceland to this day. The Althing lacked significant authority and was abolished by the Danish king in 1800. However, in 1843, a new Althing was established, if merely in a consultative form, but it claimed continuity with the original Althing of a free, independent Iceland.

Snorri Sturluson, as depicted by the Norwegian artist Christian Krohg in the 1890s.

INDEPENDENCE

Demands for home rule and independence increased during the nineteenth century as nationalists led by Jón Sigurdsson pressed for total independence. In 1874 the Althing was constitutionally guaranteed consultative status.

Home rule was introduced in 1904. Iceland became a sovereign state with its own flag in 1918, but remained subject to Denmark.

Severance from Denmark came during World War II. Iceland was of considerable strategic value to both sides. Its position in the middle of the North Atlantic made it a potentially useful base for shipping and for submarines. It could provide an airbase for planes needing to refuel while crossing the Atlantic.

In May 1940, the British occupied Iceland to preempt a German invasion and to secure this strategically important island. When the United States entered the war, the British force was replaced by sixty thousand US troops, equal to half of the population of Iceland at that time.

Icelanders resented the presence of the troops, but discovered that it brought economic benefits. Building projects, including the airport at Keflavík, provided income and jobs. Prices for Icelandic fish escalated.

The Icelandic government declared its intention to push for total independence, a move overwhelmingly approved in a national referendum. On June 17, 1944, at the traditional site of the Althing, Sveinn Björnsson, soon to become Iceland's first president, declared Iceland independent. Iceland had finally regained independence after seven hundred years.

CONTROVERSY OVER NATO AND THE US BASE

Most Icelanders want to maintain international political neutrality. Accordingly, the Althing declined US requests for ninety-nine-year leases on three bases in Iceland following World War II. In 1946 Iceland negotiated an agreement that entailed the withdrawal of US troops within six months. Permission was granted, however, for the United States to use the airbase at Keflavík.

The post-World War II beginnings of the Cold War led to the establishment of the North Atlantic Treaty Organization (NATO). Among its member nations, this mutual defense organization includes the United States, Canada, Great Britain, and most Western European countries. Iceland was persuaded to become a founding member in 1949. Membership in NATO has been a significant issue of contention between Iceland's political parties ever since. The issue was exacerbated in 1951, when US forces established a permanent marine base at the airport at Keflavík. The Icelandic government threatened to close the base in 1973 but reversed its position a year later. The issue became pressing again when contingency plans to house nuclear weapons at Keflavík were released. The Althing declared Iceland a nuclear-free zone and the United States backed down.

The US forces based in Iceland have assured Iceland's border defense for decades. However, in March 2006, the United States withdrew its bases from Iceland, effectively leaving Iceland without any armed forces. Although the United States has pledged to still defend Iceland through NATO, Norway, Denmark, Germany, and other European nations have since stepped up their defense and rescue commitment to Iceland.

Iceland is the only member of NATO to have no standing army. However, it does participate in international peacekeeping missions with the civilian-manned Icelandic Crisis Response Unit.

TWENTY-FIRST CENTURY DEVELOPMENTS

The worldwide economic crisis of 2008 hit Iceland hard. Iceland's three largest banks collapsed, causing major economic panic and chaos at home and abroad. Iceland's relationship with the United Kingdom, in particular, suffered. The British government invoked antiterrorism legislation against Iceland in order to freeze the UK-based assets of Iceland's biggest bank. That move caused a diplomatic crisis between the two nations.

Iceland took control of the banks, and appealed to the International Monetary Fund (IMF) for financial aid, which was approved. Meanwhile, Icelanders staged protests and the prime minister, Geir Haarde, resigned.

Iceland's economy and prosperity in modern times have been heavily dependent on fishing—mainly on catching cod. Iceland's only international conflicts have revolved around this industry—in particular, over the size of Iceland's exclusive offshore fishing limits.

In 1952 Iceland declared exclusive right to fish in its offshore waters for a distance of 4 miles (6.4 km) from the coast, an extension over the original 3-mile (4.8 km) fishing limit. Britain, whose fleet also fished in these waters, protested and organized a ban on importing Icelandic fish, but the expanded zone remained in force. In 1958 Iceland expanded its exclusive fishing zone to 12 miles (19.3 km), then to 50 miles (80.5 km) in 1972, and finally to 200 miles (322 km) in 1975. On each occasion, Britain protested the expansion. Both nations patrolled the waters with gunboats to enforce their point. The British deployed the Royal Navy to try to protect British trawlers, while Iceland retaliated with Fisheries' Protection Vessels. These used huge clippers to cut the nets from offending trawlers. Tensions ran high, but there were no fatalities on either side.

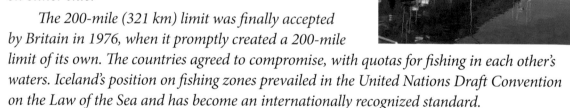

The 200-mile (321 km) limit was finally accepted by Britain in 1976, when it promptly created a 200-mile limit of its own. The countries agreed to compromise, with quotas for fishing in each other's waters. Iceland's position on fishing zones prevailed in the United Nations Draft Convention on the Law of the Sea and has become an internationally recognized standard.

Iceland's 200-mile limit created an overlap in the Barents Sea known as the "Herring loophole" with Norway's offshore limit. An agreement was reached on this area in 1980, but conflicts over the precise scope of each country's limits dragged on for years until Iceland, Norway, and Russia signed an agreement in 1999 letting Iceland fish in Russia's and Norway's Exclusive Economic Zone in exchange for certain benefits on Icelandic waters. Iceland, together with the United Kingdom and Ireland, is also in an ongoing dispute with Denmark over the latter's claim that the Faroe Islands' fisheries extend beyond the 200-mile line, disputing the Danish fishing boats' rights to operate in the area.

Johanna Sigurdardottir became the new prime minister in 2009—the country's first woman prime minister and the first openly gay head of government. She favored having Iceland become a member of the European Union (EU) and her administration took steps to begin the process.

With the support of the IMF, the Icelandic government imposed strict economic controls and jailed some of the bankers whose misdeeds had contributed to the collapse. In 2015, the IMF found that Iceland had made a strong recovery from the crisis with particularly robust performances in tourism, energy, and fisheries. A new government, elected in 2013, did not want Iceland to join the EU and withdrew the country's application for membership in 2015.

In 2016, a scandal forced Prime Minister Sigmundur David Gunnlaugsson from office. Documents leaked from a Panamanian law firm, informally called the "Panama Papers," revealed the names and hidden assets of thousands of wealthy people, including the prime minister and his wife, among many other high-profile world officials. Sigurdur Ingi Johannsson took over as prime minister in April 2016, and Gudni Thorlacius Johannesson became president in August 2016.

INTERNET LINKS

news.bbc.co.uk/2/hi/europe/country_profiles/1025288.stm
The BBC News site provides a chronology of key events in Icelandic history.

www.extremeiceland.is/en/information/about-iceland/history-of-iceland
This website provides a detailed history of Iceland.

www.sagamuseum.is
The website of this Reykjavik museum tells stories of some important figures from Iceland's earliest years.

GOVERNMENT

The Icelandic parliament building in Reykjavik dates to 1881.

3

N 930 CE, A GROUP OF SETTLERS gathered on the plains by the River Oxara in southwestern Iceland to establish the law of the new nation. This assembly of early Icelanders continued to meet for two weeks each summer to create laws, resolve disputes, and air grievances and concerns. The meeting place came to be called Thingvellir ("Parliament Fields"), and the assembly of lawmakers became the *Alþingi* (Althing, sometimes spelled Althingi). Today that field is part of Thingvellir National Park, and the Althing continues as the world's oldest functioning parliament.

Despite that noble democratic beginning, Iceland spent most of its history as a colony, first of Norway, and later, of Denmark. Iceland began its steps toward independence in the early twentieth century, with Denmark granting it home rule in 1904. The present Icelandic constitution and institutions of government date from the declaration of independence in 1944. Today, Iceland is a healthy, stable democratic nation.

"Pride in the strong association of the Alþing to medieval Norse/Germanic governance, known through the twelfth century Icelandic sagas and reinforced during the fight for independence in the nineteenth century, have, together with the powerful natural setting of the assembly grounds, given the (Þingvellir National Park) site iconic status as a shrine for the national Icelandic identity."
—UNESCO World Heritage Center

STRUCTURE OF GOVERNMENT

Iceland's president
Gudni Johannesson
in 2016.

As a parliamentary republic, Iceland is governed by an elected president and an elected parliament headed by a prime minister. All citizens over eighteen are entitled to vote both for the president and members of parliament.

The president of Iceland is the head of state, primarily a constitutional figurehead. Gudni Thorlacius Johannesson, a historian, became the president in August 2016. He is unaffiliated with any of Iceland's political parties. A president is elected for a four-year term and may stand for reelection. He or she represents the country but is much less powerful than, for example, the president of the United States. The president of Iceland cannot simply veto legislation passed by parliament, but can reject a piece of legislation and send it on to a referendum. Rather than participating in day-to-day politics, the president acts as a unifying figure.

The prime minister is the head of government. The current prime minister, in 2016, is Sigurdur Ingi Johannsson of the Progressive Party. (He is also a veterinarian.) The prime minister is the leading political figure, like the prime minister of most Western European countries. He or she heads the cabinet, which is currently a group of twelve ministers in charge of ten ministries. These ministries are the Ministries of Finance and Economic Affairs; Health; Education; Industry and Trade; Social Affairs and Housing; Foreign Affairs; the Interior; Environmental and Natural Resources; and Fisheries and Agriculture.

Parliament is known as the Althing to maintain continuity with the earliest parliament. The Althing, which meets in Reykjavik, consists of sixty-three members elected to four-year terms through a mixture of constituency and proportional representation. The Althing enacts all legislation and passes the annual budget.

In addition to national representation, there are also elected officials at the regional and local levels. Local government carries most of the responsibility for education, municipal services, and health services. It also looks after the unemployed and poor through job-creation programs.

PARTY POLITICS

Iceland has a multiparty political system. There is a tradition of coalition governments since one party rarely has enough representatives to give it an overall majority in government. Parties come and go, but some of the largest parties currently include the following:

Sigurdur Johannsson, Iceland's prime minister in 2016.

- **Progressive Party**—center right, liberal, Nordic agrarian, Eurosceptic (opposes the EU) party, pro-NATO
- **Social Democratic Alliance**—center left, feminist, pro-Europeanist (favors EU), eco-socialist
- **Independence Party**—center right, liberal conservative, Eurosceptic party, pro-NATO
- **Left-Green Movement**—left, Democratic socialist, eco-socialist, pro-Europeanist
- **Bright Future**—center, social liberalism, green, pro-European, staunchly neutral in foreign affairs

THE WOMEN'S ALLIANCE

Women's issues rose to prominence in the Althing due to the existence of *Kvennalista* (KVEN-eh-list-eh), the Women's List or the Women's Alliance. This party was formed before the 1983 election to press for action on issues such as child care and equal opportunity for women. It won three deputies in the Althing. In keeping with the egalitarian ideals of the party, there was no formal leadership: the role of parliamentary leader rotated among its elected deputies.

Prime Minister
David
Gunnlaugsson
addresses
a session of
parliament in
April 2016.

Despite the existence of Kvennalista, in 1995 only one cabinet position was held by a woman. This caused an uproar and the ruling Independence Party assigned four women cabinet ministers the following term. Although the Kvennalista disbanded in 1999, its remaining members have since formed the Alliance coalition.

A WELFARE STATE

Certain minimum guarantees for public welfare are provided for in the Constitution of Iceland. Articles 70 and 71 read: "Whoever is unable to provide for himself or his dependants shall, subject to duties prescribed by law, be entitled to support from public funds, unless his maintenance rests upon others. If parents cannot afford to educate their children, or if the children are orphaned or destitute, their education and maintenance must be defrayed from public funds."

The state provides old-age and disability pensions for the elderly and infirm, along with benefits for childbearing and for sickness. Ninety percent of Icelandic workers belong to unions, which offer benefits such as guaranteed support in the event of unemployment.

Health insurance is compulsory for all citizens and all medical and hospital services are provided entirely without charge. The rate of infant mortality in Iceland is the lowest in the world, and an effective public health-care system helps to contribute to the longevity of the Icelandic population. Women have an average life expectancy, in 2016, of 85.22 years and men of 80.81, both of which are almost the highest in the world.

INTERNET LINKS

www.cia.gov/library/publications/the-world-factbook/geos/ic.html
The CIA World Factbook has up-to-date information about the Icelandic government.

eng.forsaetisraduneyti.is
This is the site of the prime minister's office, in English.

www.government.is
This is the official site of the Icelandic government, which is available in English. It has links to the constitution and the site of the Althing.

whc.unesco.org/en/list/1152
The World Heritage listing of Thingvellir National Park explains the creation and importance of the Althing.

ECONOMY

The Icelandic currency is the *krona* (plural is *kronur*).
The 500 kronur bill is the smallest banknote now in
circulation. Coins are the 100, 50, 10, 5, and 1 krona (kr).

4

CELAND'S ECONOMY IS SIMILAR TO those in other Scandinavian countries. It combines capitalism and free-market principles with an extensive welfare system. For the most part, this system works well for Iceland, which boasts a healthy, growing economy, low unemployment, and a remarkably even distribution of income. The global economic crisis of 2008 hit Iceland very hard, making worldwide headlines when its three largest banks failed, but its recovery has been rapid and robust.

The economy depends heavily on the fishing industry, and the export of aluminum, and ferrosilicon. Since 2010, tourism has become the main pillar of Icelandic economic growth, and the number of tourists annually continues to soar. Iceland has also been diversifying into manufacturing and service industries in the last decade. In addition to tourism, which employed 21,600 people in 2014, the growing sectors include software production and biotechnology.

Iceland's other major resource is its vast supply of geothermal energy. This can be tapped in various ways, from heating homes to providing cheap energy for factories. The natural beauty of the island also makes it an obvious site for tourism.

The popular HBO fantasy series *Game of Thrones* was partly filmed in Iceland, showcasing some of the country's astonishing natural beauty. This sparked so much interest that now some tourism companies offer special *Game of Thrones* tours to filming locations on the island.

COST OF LIVING

The cost of living in Iceland is very high. Most goods have to be imported and the tiny size of the population means that there are no economies of scale. Iceland's extensive social services are supported by high taxation, which further drives up the cost of living.

Despite the high cost of living, Icelanders generally buy many high-priced goods and live an affluent lifestyle. Most people own cell phones and personal computers, and almost everyone—more than 98.2 percent of Icelanders—is connected to the internet.

Icelanders support their high standard of living by working long and hard; they put in the longest workweek in Europe. Some 82 percent of Icelandic women work outside the home. Unemployment has traditionally been very low, with a rate of 3.8 percent in 2015.

FISHING

The economic life of Iceland still depends on fish. Although fishing and fish processing employ only about 5 percent of the labor force, fish products provide 40 percent of Iceland's exports. The major fish catches are cod and haddock—exported either frozen, salted, or fresh—and capelin and herring, which are usually reduced to oil and meal.

Icelanders sell their fish to markets in North America and Europe. Nutrition studies stressing the health benefits of a fish diet that is naturally high in protein and low in cholesterol have helped ensure high demand.

However, intensive modern fishing methods have threatened Iceland's fish stocks. The government acted to protect stocks through an expansion of the exclusive fishing zone, now at 200 nautical miles (370.4 km), to prevent overfishing by rival nations.

It also imposed strict quotas. Icelandic vessels are given quotas based on the previous year's catch and the government's assessment of fish stocks of each species. These quotas are tradable, which has made fishermen develop the skills of futures traders who need to speculate with the canniness of accountants.

Iceland's waters are very rich in fish because many different species breed where the cold waters of the Arctic mix with the warm waters of the Gulf Stream. The different varieties of fish can be categorized by the environment in which they live in the ocean. Icelandic fishing fleets catch such bottom-feeding fish as cod, haddock, redfish, ocean catfish, Greenland halibut, and plaice, and top-water fish such as herring and capelin. They also catch fish that are on their way to freshwater rivers to breed, such as salmon, trout, and Arctic char. Shellfish such as shrimps, scallops, and Norway lobsters are also part of the catch.

Iceland's fishing fleet is among the most modern and efficient in the world. Icelandic fisheries are deeply committed to sustainable practices and protecting the marine ecosystem and biodiversity, based on scientific guidance from the Icelandic Marine Research Institute. The government's Directorate of Fisheries provides ongoing oversight and enforcement.

WHALING

Whaling traditionally occupied a significant part of Iceland's economy. The whales were harpooned and brought to whale-processing stations on the coast, where the blubber was stripped and the carcass processed into meat and oil.

As whale stocks became overexploited in the 1980s, the International Whaling Commission called for a voluntary temporary moratorium on all whaling. Iceland, however, along with Japan, insisted on continuing with limited whaling. As public sentiment through most of the world turned in favor of a complete cessation of whaling, Iceland (and Japan and Norway) became more isolated because of their pro-whaling stance. In the mid-1980s environmental activists belonging to Greenpeace took direct action against the whaling industry: they sank an Icelandic ship and destroyed other whaling equipment.

Most Icelanders were appalled by this act of deliberate sabotage. Fishermen resented having their livelihood taken away because of what

In 2009, a whaling boat pulls two fin whales alongside it in the waters off Hvalfjsrour on Iceland's western coast.

they considered sentimental attachment to an animal. City dwellers were more likely to be sympathetic to whales, but still resented foreign meddling in Icelandic affairs. Nevertheless, US boycotts of Icelandic fish products threatened to do real damage to the Icelandic economy and encouraged a moderation of Iceland's whaling position.

Although Iceland still believes it has the right to conduct whaling in its waters, it guaranteed to restrict whaling operations to "research whaling," in which whaling was conducted only for scientific purposes and most of the products from the whales were not exported for commercial purposes. In 1989, however, even this limited whaling was suspended. Fourteen years later, controversy arose over the government's decision to conduct scientific whaling to investigate the impact of whales on fish stocks.

In 2006, Iceland resumed commercial whaling with quotas set and permits issued for scientific catches. To the grave concern of environmental groups, the government allows the hunting of fin whales, which are endangered. Much of the catch is exported to Japan, as most Icelanders no longer eat whale meat. However, the pressure of tourism keeps demands high in Iceland as well, as tourists expect to eat whale as part of their perception of an Icelandic experience, and many restaurants are happy to provide it.

Whales have sporadically stranded themselves on Icelandic beaches since earliest times. These beachings were considered a significant windfall for a district. Local farmers would descend on the whale and flense it—that is, remove the blubber from the skeleton. The blubber was cut into strips, which were hung under a bridge or from the eaves of a house. The meat would be left to mature, turning black, until it was ready to eat.

There would often be disputes over who had a right to a beached whale. Legally, such drift-finds were the property of the owner of the land. In Grettir's Saga, such a dispute arises while the finders are flensing a fin whale discovered at Rifsker. The dispute turns nasty:

"Thorgeir Bottleback was the first to get on to the whale where Flósi's men were. Thorfinn was cutting it up, standing near the head on the place where he had been carving. 'Here I bring you your ax,' said Thorgeir. Then he struck at Thorfinn's neck and cut off his head."

The following verse was composed about these events:

Hard were the blows which were dealt at Rifsker;
No weapons they had but steaks of the whale.
They belabored each other with rotten blubber.
Unseemly methinks is such warfare for men.

FARMING

Iceland began as an agricultural nation, but today only 4.8 percent of Icelanders are employed on farms, and agriculture accounts for only 5.8 percent of the Icelandic economy. Nevertheless, many Icelanders have a nostalgic fondness for farming, recalling a time earlier in the twentieth century when most people lived and worked on farms. Sheep farming is the most important agricultural industry in the country, and dairy farming is also significant.

The short growing season of the northern climate limits the kinds of vegetables than will grow in Iceland. Root vegetables including potatoes, turnips, and carrots along with hardy plants such as cabbage, cauliflower, and kale, can be grown outdoors. Other crops, such as tomatoes, cucumbers, and peppers, as well as cut flowers and potted plants, are grown in greenhouses heated by geothermal energy. Practically all fruit, along with other vegetables, has to be imported.

THERMAL ENERGY

The geological activity that is so visible throughout Iceland represents a potential economic resource and creates a setting of stark beauty. Iceland has harnessed various forms of geothermal energy to provide cheap heat and power for homes and industry. The Reykjavik municipality currently uses this inexpensive, clean form of energy to provide central heating for all city households. Since most heat is tapped from seismic activity beneath the earth's surface, it is not necessary to burn much oil or other hydrocarbons as fuel, thus no environmentally harmful greenhouse gases are produced. All the same, only a small fraction of potentially exploitable geothermal power is currently harnessed.

Iceland's rivers provide hydroelectric power, but only a small fraction of the energy that could be exploited has been developed. In view of the potential for further clean electricity production through geothermal and hydroelectric generation, there is currently a plan to export electricity to Europe. This involves an ambitious plan to build the longest submarine electric cable in

THE NOT-QUITE MYTH OF ICELANDIC BANANA PRODUCTION

According to an urban myth that still surfaces on the internet, Iceland is Europe's largest producer of bananas. It's not true and never was. However, the myth does contain a shred of truth. Iceland does in fact grow bananas, and has since 1941. The bananas are grown in greenhouses powered by geothermal energy. From 1945 to about 1960, they were produced for commercial purposes for the domestic market.

In 1960, the Icelandic government removed import duties on fruit and the price of imported bananas came down. In fact, the greenhouse-grown domestic varieties couldn't compete, pricewise, with the imported bananas, so commercial production ceased.

Nevertheless, a small number of bananas are still grown in a greenhouse by the Agricultural University of Iceland. The school also grows coffee, cocoa, and avocadoes. The fruits are consumed by students and staff but aren't sold.

The Blue Lagoon is a famous tourist attraction formed by the geothermal power plant seen in this view.

the world under the Atlantic Ocean from Iceland to Britain at an estimated cost of $6.6 billion, a project that is still in the discussion stage between the two countries.

One geothermal project near Keflavík has had a surprising spin-off. Superheated salt water is pumped from deep in the earth and used to generate electricity. It then passes through a heat exchanger to provide hot fresh water for heating homes. The mineral-rich saltwater from the earth finally runs off into a pool named the Blue Lagoon. Those who bathe in these warm waters claim to have been cured of various skin complaints.

TOURISM

In the nineteenth century, Iceland was an exotic destination for European travelers, and many of them wrote accounts of their travels. Tourism has become increasingly popular and now constitutes a significant part of Iceland's economic activity. In 1950, 4,000 tourists visited Iceland; in 2015, there were 1,261,938 visitors, a number that greatly exceeds the population of Iceland. Most visitors come from the United States, the United Kingdom, and Germany.

Tourists are brought to Iceland by Icelandair, the national airline and other airlines. The other way of getting there is by car ferry from Denmark, Norway, Scotland, or the Faroe Islands.

Tourists are drawn above all by the natural beauty of the island and by the resonance of its historic sites. Three of the major tourist sites—the site of the early parliament at Thingvellir, the Gullfoss waterfall, and the active geysers around Geysir—are easily accessible from Reykjavik.

Iceland is particularly suited to outdoor pursuits. Hikers walk in the unpopulated interior. Equestrians explore on Iceland's distinctive small horses. And people relax after their exertions by swimming in the pools heated by geothermal water.

Recreational fishing is popular in Icelandic rivers but is regulated to preserve fish stocks and maximize revenue.

Another expanding area for tourism is the opportunity to live on a farm. "Tourist farming" has been embraced by some farmers as an additional opportunity for diversification. As Icelandic farms become less economic for producing food, farmers are able to capitalize on the nostalgia for a rural lifestyle by opening up their farms to tourists who pay to take part in such activities as rounding up the sheep.

In recent times, Iceland has been marketing itself as an ideal "green" tourist and whale-watching destination. The island's particularly clean air and water and the use of geothermal energy rather than the burning of hydrocarbons is a source of pride for Icelanders. The government has stated its objective "that Iceland be, by the turn of the century, the cleanest country in the Western world and that an image of cleanliness and sustainability be associated with all developments."

INTERNET LINKS

www.mnn.com/lifestyle/eco-tourism/blogs/icelandic-tourism-trough-roof-and-s-not-necessarily-good-thing
Mother Nature Network offers a very good article on the effect of the tourism boom on Iceland.

modernfarmer.com/2014/11/frozen-banana-republic
This article, with good photos, discusses Iceland's banana production as well as the geothermal resources that enable it.

us.whales.org/issues/whaling-in-iceland
This conservation site discusses concerns about whaling in Iceland, including statistics.

ENVIRONMENT

People on a whale-watching tour boat get a treat near Husavik City in Iceland.

GIVEN THE SMALL NUMBER OF people who live in Iceland, it's not surprising that pollution is not as great a problem as it is in many other countries. Nevertheless, conservation of the environment is a major concern, particularly in certain areas. The country is very reliant on the fishing industry, for example, and therefore, sustainable fisheries and care of ocean resources is a top priority for both economic and environmental reasons. Other areas of particular interest for Iceland's environmentalists are wind erosion and desertification, deforestation, energy production, and the increasing burden of tourism.

The number of tourists has skyrocketed in recent years to some four times the national population, and most tourists visit the same few places. Many of those are natural sites that are environmentally very sensitive to such an impact. In addition, the huge influx of people brings added waste products to a system that cannot manage it all.

In reference to the fact that global warming is melting the country's iconic glaciers at an alarming rate, one resident is said to have quipped, "Without ice, Iceland is just land."

A house in the small
fishing village of
Djupivogur sits
very close to shore.

Some Icelanders are sounding alarm bells. The government naturally wants to encourage tourism, but has yet to conduct any studies on its environmental impact.

MARINE CONSERVATION

The coastal zones of Iceland are of great economic value as Iceland depends heavily on fishing. The majority of Icelanders also live near the coast, so the preservation of Iceland's waters is a sound social and economic move. Iceland does not suffer from much water pollution as laws and regulations ensure that pollution is kept to a minimum.

There are numerous environmental bodies in charge of protection and conservation of marine resources for sustainable use. Although there is no marine ecosystem currently in danger, checks are already in place to preempt an ecological imbalance. The relevant bodies make sure that the dumping of waste products off fishing fleets, oil spills, and the transportation

WHERE ARE THE TREES?

There was a time, long ago, when birch forests covered 25 to 40 percent of Iceland. When the settlers first arrived more than one thousand years ago, they used those trees to build houses and burn for warmth and cooking. They also cut down forests and burned scrubland to create pastureland for sheep. The grazing animals prevented the woods from regenerating, and eventually, Iceland was essentially left barren of forests. About 95 percent of the original forest cover was permanently destroyed.

Well into the twentieth century, Icelanders were still felling what few wooded areas remained for fuel. By mid-century, less than 0.5 to 1 percent of the country's land area was forested. Even today, the island's large numbers of sheep prevent woodlands from rebounding.

Over time, some Icelanders came to believe that the island's climate prevented the growth of trees. But that was never the case. Beginning in 1899, some people began to try to recover some portion of their forests. The Iceland Forest Service (IFS) was established in 1908, and continues today, along with dozens of local forestry societies. Their goals are to plan, plant, and cultivate new forests for economic, ecological, and recreational purposes. In 2014, about 2 percent of Iceland was covered by forest. By the year 2100, forestry officials aim to have 12 percent of the island once again supporting woodlands.

Trees grow in greenhouses heated by geothermal energy from the town of Egilsstadir in northeast Iceland.

Iceland is growing taller. That's one surprising result of global warming, according to a 2015 report by geologists at the University of Arizona. Iceland is losing about 11 billion tons (about 10 billion t) of ice per year due to climate change. As the glaciers melt, their reduced weight relieves pressure on the earth's crust beneath them. The ground essentially rebounds like a memory foam mattress.

Iceland is springing up about 1.4 inches (3.5 cm) a year, and will probably speed up as more ice melts. By 2025, scientists predict, the rate could be a much as 1.6 inches (4 cm) a year, which is about the same growth rate as an elementary-school child. Though not noticeable to the human eye, the increased movement of the bedrock will probably cause more volcanoes and earthquakes.

of hazardous chemicals are kept tightly in check. Even the types of fishing gear and mesh sizes of nets used are strictly regulated. Quotas are imposed to prevent overfishing and penalties are levied for illegal catches. This is to prevent the depletion of fish stocks, especially since particular species of fish of high commercial value tended to be overfished.

Currently there are four types of protected areas in the coastal zone. Depending on the area, trawl fishing is prohibited in protected coastal waters. Protected areas may also be closed off for long periods to protect young fishes, certain species of fish, or the ecosystem. During the spawning season, the area may be closed off for a short period of time. If the Marine Research Institute sees fit, it can also cordon off certain areas to prevent damage to fishing stocks and ecosystems.

GLOBAL WARMING

In late 2004, more than two hundred scientists and researchers from the Arctic Council released an alarming report on rising temperatures in the Arctic. The increase in the earth's average temperature, or global warming, is largely due to the burning of fossil fuels, which releases greenhouse gases. According to the report, there had been an increase in the water levels in the Arctic because of melting ice caps. In the previous thirty years, almost

An explorer takes
a photograph
inside a cave at the
Vatnajokull glacier.

386,100 square miles (999,995 square km) of sea ice had melted and the average winter temperature of the Arctic today had increased by 35.6°F (2°C) compared to a century ago. Observations since the release of that report have confirmed its basic findings, although some changes are happening faster and are more significant than originally foreseen.

Vatnajokull, the largest glacier in southeast Iceland, is fast receding due to global warming. Melting at the rate of 3 feet (1 m) annually, Vatnajokull could completely disappear in the next three hundred years. Approximately 11 percent of Iceland is covered in glacial ice and permanent snow and 3,088 miles (4,970 km) of coastal waters surrounds Iceland. If global warming were to continue unchecked, the subsequent rise in water levels and melting of ice caps would be detrimental to Iceland.

Iceland ratified the Kyoto Protocol in 2002 limiting emissions of greenhouse gases. Further steps that Iceland hopes to take include boosting public transportation and limiting the number of private cars on the road. This is particularly important as heavy traffic in the Greater Reykjavik area is a cause of air pollution. Iceland also hopes to reduce the dependence on fossil fuels for the operation of its fishing vessels. Further technological research and developments in the field of clean sources of energy are necessary to help tackle the problem of global warming.

THE IMPORTANCE OF RENEWABLE ENERGY

There are abundant renewable energy resources like hydropower and geothermal energy in Iceland. Geothermal energy, used primarily for heating purposes, makes up about 65 percent and hydropower, used for generating electricity, makes up 20 percent of Iceland's energy use. The rest comes from imported fossil fuels. Today there are five major geothermal plants and nine hydropower plants.

Geothermal energy is used to power homes, greenhouses, and industry, and supply warm water for fish farming and swimming pools. This form of energy, however, produces wastewater containing hazardous chemicals like boron, mercury, and arsenic, which if not disposed of properly, could pollute Iceland's waters.

A geothermal power station steams on a cold day in Iceland.

However, the benefits of using geothermal energy far outweigh the negative effects. Compared to nuclear power plants, geothermal plants do not deplete the ozone layer and have little negative impact on the environment if properly managed.

The largest hydroelectric stations make use of the flow of Iceland's glacial rivers, while numerous smaller hydropower plants are located on clear-water streams and rivers throughout the country.

Iceland's first wind power turbines became operational in 2013. However, electricity generated by wind power is still not cost effective compared to hydro and geothermal sources; however that could change in time.

Only around 20 to 25 percent of Iceland's potential sources for renewable energy are presently being utilized. Many future projects have been planned, but some may never be built because of environmental concerns and public objections.

WASTE

Iceland has made slow but considerable progress in waste management. In the 1970s it was common to incinerate waste in an open pit and smoky open dumps were a common sight. In the 1990s, incineration became less popular, with only 1.2 percent of waste being incinerated. Uncontrolled open pit burning was gradually stopped by the year 2000 as recycling became a more environmentally conscious option.

On the other hand, the use of landfills as a method for waste management is still in use. In 2016, 50 percent of all household waste in Iceland was still being sent to landfills, a much higher proportion than in neighboring countries. Nevertheless, landfill use is falling steadily.

There are no recycling facilities in Iceland, so glass waste is buried in landfills. Other recyclable items are shipped abroad for processing. Plastics go to Sweden for sorting, and from there, to other countries for recycling. Paper waste is shipped to Holland for sorting and then onward as well. Metal materials are also sent abroad. Hazardous waste, likewise, must be shipped overseas. Radioactive waste, however, is not an issue as there are no nuclear power plants in Iceland.

Barrow's goldeneye ducklings sit on the shore of the Laxa River in Myvatn, Iceland.

PROTECTED AREAS

Much of Iceland's nature and wildlife habitat is under conservation and protection. There are 3 national parks and 102 protected areas in Iceland. The parks are Thingvellir National Park, founded in 1930; Snaefellsjökull National Park, created in 2001; and Vatnajokull National Park, created in 2008. This park, which encompasses the Vatnajokull glacier, also incorporates two previous national parks, Skaftafell and Jokulsargljufur, into one larger park. Vatnajokull National Park now covers 5,374 square miles (13,920 sq km), about 14 percent of Iceland, and is Europe's second largest national park after Yugyd Va in Russia.

Some of the protected areas include Myvatn, Gullfoss, and Surtsey among others. These parks are designed to keep Iceland's wildlife safe, conserve the area's unique landscape, and, at the same time, offer tourists and Icelanders alike a glimpse of Iceland's natural wilderness.

At the Myvatn-Laxa Nature Conservation Area, a lake region in the north of the country, there are numerous duck species, including the tufted duck, the scaup, Barrow's goldeneye, and other rare species like the goosander, shoveller, and pochard. In Iceland, all endangered or rare birds, like the gyrfalcon and the white-tailed eagle, are protected by law. In 1926 there were only ten pairs of white-tailed eagles in Iceland. Today there are about seventy-five breeding pairs. Permission from the Ministry of Culture is needed if one wishes to photograph or approach the endangered birds' nesting places.

The conservation and protection of nature is important to Icelanders. Conservationists petitioned against a project to build a new aluminium smelter in eastern Iceland. They were concerned that the project would destroy the landscape. The Karahnukar hydropower plant project has so far dammed two major glacial rivers north of Vatnajokull. The Icelandic Nature Conservation Association campaigned hard for the conservation of this area but this controversial project still proceeded. The construction of a new plant in Iceland will always be a source of contention and the benefits of progress must outweigh the cost to Iceland's environment. Iceland will have to balance the twin goals of full utilization of its natural resources with the preservation of its land and sea.

INTERNET LINKS

grapevine.is/mag/feature/2016/08/12/feature
Stunning photos of Iceland's highlands are interspersed with commentary about the need to protect the region from industrial development.

www.iceland.is/the-big-picture/nature-environment/environment
This official Iceland site offers information about the environment, natural resources, and links to related sites.

news.nationalgeographic.com/news/2014/08/140827-seabird-puffin-tern-iceland-ocean-climate-change-science-winged-warning
This article warns of a massive die-off of Iceland's seabird population.

www.skogur.is/english/forestry-in-a-treeless-land
This in-depth article traces the history of deforestation and the current state of forestry in Iceland.

ust.is/the-environment-agency-of-iceland
The Environment Agency of Iceland's site includes a good amount of information in English.

ICELANDERS

A couple wears typical Icelandic woolen sweaters.

6

GENETIC ANALYSIS OF DNA LINEAGE confirms what was already well known about the people of Iceland. They are largely the descendents of people from Scandinavia, Scotland, and Ireland. The original settlers were a mix of Nordic Vikings and Celtic slaves and wives. After a millennium of relative isolation and intermarriage, no distinctions between the two groups are evident any longer. As such, the population is quite homogeneous. The population is essentially Nordic in appearance: characteristically tall, blond-haired, and light-skinned.

A HOMOGENOUS SOCIETY

Historically, there have been virtually no racial minorities in Iceland. In general, immigration into Iceland is heavily restricted and the number of immigrants has been very small. In the past, the largest number of immigrants came from other Nordic countries and have not contributed to diversifying the ethnic makeup of the country.

"One cannot overemphasize, I think, how very, very few Icelanders there actually are. If they were an animal species, they would be on the World Wildlife Fund's endangered list—the human equivalent of a yellow-nosed albatross. It's remarkable that they have been able to build any kind of a national infrastructure at all."
—Michael Booth, *The Almost Nearly Perfect People*, 2016

The same is true of literature. Iceland has the highest concentration of bookstores per capita in the world. A remarkable number of Icelanders are poets and novelists. It's said that 10 percent of them will publish a book.

Icelanders keep abreast of current affairs and tend to be well-informed about international affairs. They also tend to travel abroad widely.

NATIONALISM

Icelanders have a strong sense of nationalism. They are conscious of their small population size, of the tangential place of their island in world affairs, and of the threat of being overwhelmed by the dominant cultures of the United States or Europe. There is a sense of pride about the distinctiveness of their ways and their ability to prosper despite the rigors of climate and geography. They also look proudly on their long heritage of unusual achievement.

Icelandic nationalism is apparent in various international forums. Joining NATO has been controversial because the alliance contradicts Iceland's firm stance of neutrality. Iceland has resisted joining the European Union because some Icelanders think doing so would threaten their independence.

Icelandic nationalism was evident in the expansion of the Icelandic fishing zones. During the Cod Wars, feelings against Britain ran high. The same attitude is implicit in Icelanders' reluctance to accept the ban on whaling.

TRADITION AND DRESS

Icelanders have a lively sense of tradition. This is fostered by an interest in personal genealogy. The medieval sagas are still popular reading in Iceland today. During a festival like Thorrablót, Icelanders like to sample traditional foods. Similarly, traditional dress is worn by some people on a festival like Independence Day.

Icelanders today dress much like most Americans or Europeans. Indeed, many Icelanders are very fashion conscious. Designer-label clothes sell well in Reykjavik as Icelanders love to dress up on a Friday or Saturday night.

Iceland's most distinctive contribution to fashion lies in knitwear. Icelanders still wear heavy sweaters in traditional designs made from

Icelandic wool. These sweaters are traditionally made in white or earth tones with a decorative design around the yoke. They are effective for keeping Icelanders warm in the cold weather.

Traditional national costumes have been revived by the Reykjavik Folk-Dancing Society and as part of the Independence Day festivities. Women wear a black skirt of homespun cloth and a black knitted cardigan with a high neckline, long sleeves, and a white shirt underneath. Fancy dresses might have used such imported material as linen, velvet, and silk. Such a dress would be completed with a silk neckerchief like a cravat, and a waist belt. Most striking of all is the headwear: either a knitted cap with a tassel or a tall white cascading headdress. The men's traditional dress consists of a dark-colored tunic and breeches tucked into long socks. Men, too, wear cravat-like neckerchiefs and distinctive headgear: long conical woolen caps.

INTERNET LINKS

buningurinn.is/english
The Icelandic National Costume Board offers a good slideshow with English sidebars.

www.iom.int/world-migration
An interactive map on this site identifies the numbers and countries of origin of Iceland's immigrants, as well as the places where Icelanders live abroad.

www.irishtimes.com/news/why-people-in-iceland-look-just-like-us-1.1104676
This article in the *Irish Times* discusses the genetic origins of Iceland's people.

wsimag.com/fashion/8127-the-icelandic-national-costume
The *Wall Street Journal* has an interesting article about Icelandic traditional clothing.

LIFESTYLE

Hikers enjoy a beautiful view at Landmannalaugar in the Highlands of Iceland.

ICELANDERS WORK HARD AND PLAY hard. Children as young as twelve begin working during the summer. Many adults hold two jobs. Icelanders work a longer week, in terms of hours, than people in most other industrialized nations. All this is required to earn money for spending on the good things that Icelanders enjoy in abundance—fashionable clothes, consumer goods, travel, and cultural events.

The Icelandic environment probably plays a major, if unquantifiable, part in forming the national lifestyle. The long dark winters may well encourage a tendency to party and drink, as well as to enjoy music, read, and write. The long days of summer may play some part in explaining Icelanders' intense energy, evident both in their work and play. The very bleakness of the elements in Iceland may encourage both a sense of self-sufficiency and also a sense of community.

Icelanders live in a stark but beautiful setting where they have to struggle against the natural elements of earthquakes and glaciers, rough seas and swollen rivers, cold weather and long periods of darkness. However, there are no problems of pollution, no army, and no tradition of militarism. People work very hard, but in return enjoy a very high standard of living and do not face significant unemployment.

Icelandic society is small and cohesive, which means that it lacks diversity and can seem oppressively normative, but this also helps

Iceland's very low marriage rate spurred a widely circulated hoax on the internet. In 2016, an article went viral stating that the Icelandic government would pay $5,000 a month to immigrants who married Icelandic women, and that priority would go to North Africans. Many Icelandic women said they were bombarded with marriage proposals from foreign men on social media. Of course, the report was completely bogus.

People walk and shop on a sunny April day in Reykjavik.

it to be relatively classless and crimefree. Icelandic culture mythologizes the independent-spirited individual, but Icelanders also value family and community.

THE WORK WEEK

Although the Icelandic standard legal work week is forty hours, the average work week actually amounts to forty-seven hours for men and thirty-seven hours for women. That is easily the longest in Europe, and many Icelanders put in additional overtime. Some even take on a second job. However, in recent years, members of parliament have proposed a thirty-five-hour work week, in order to provide a better work-life balance for most Icelanders.

Icelanders on the whole are very responsible about work. They tend to take it seriously and both expect and are expected to work hard. Indeed, during the British occupation of World War II, Icelanders looked down on working for the British because such work was considered too easy, with too short a workday and too little commitment required.

THE ROLE OF WOMEN

According to the World Economic Forum (WEF), Iceland is the best place on earth to be a woman. That is, the annual WEF Global Gender Gap Report ranked Iceland number 1 out of 145 countries in the years 2009 to 2015. Iceland's 2015 score is 0.881, in which 1.0 indicates full equality and 0.0 equals complete inequality. (For comparison, the United States ranked 28 with a score of 0.740.)

From 1980 to 1996, Iceland had a woman president, and in 2009, its first female prime minister took office. Also that year, the Althing achieved an even representation of men and women, although the ratio changes with each new government.

Prostitution and strip clubs, regarded in Iceland as forms of human trafficking in which women are disproportionately treated as commodities for sale, were outlawed in 2009 and 2010.

Iceland's prime minister Johanna Sigurdardottir listens to speakers at a 2011 meeting in London.

Within the home, Icelandic women still bear a disproportionate burden of domestic work. Women are more likely to cook the meals for a family and to bear primary responsibility for looking after the children.

MARRIAGE

As in the other Nordic countries, marriage in Iceland has become a very optional institution for couples. In 2011, the marriage rate fell to 4.6 per 1,000 people, nearly its lowest level ever. (In 1990, it was 4.5 per 1,000.) For comparison, in 2010, the US marriage rate was 6.8 per 1,000 people, which represented the lowest level ever for the United States. Same-sex marriage became legal in Iceland in 2010.

Many Icelandic couples do not get married until they can afford their own house or apartment. Those who go on to university do not graduate until they are at least twenty-four years old. In 2013, about 38 percent of Icelanders in their twenties were living with their parents. Young couples may also live with one set of parents. They may choose to have their first child, even though they may have no plans to get married yet.

The actual wedding ceremony of Icelanders is similar to that in the United States, with church weddings being quite common. If the couple already has children, they are incorporated into the ceremony as flower-bearers or similar assistants. A honeymoon abroad is an attractive prospect but is sufficiently expensive that many young couples often have to delay it until they are fully established at work.

BIRTH AND PARENTHOOD

In 2014, 70.5 percent of Icelandic babies were born to parents who were not married. In fact, Iceland leads the world in the percentage of children born outside marriage. In some countries, being a single parent is an economic burden; and in some places, it carries a social stigma—but not in Iceland.

Social support systems are so strong that single parenthood has become the norm. For one thing, Iceland guarantees some of the most generous parental leave in the world—nine months at 80 percent pay for new parents. That breaks down to three months for mom, three for dad, and another three to be divided between them as they wish. Parental time off also applies to adoption, foster parenting, and some miscarriages and stillbirths. There is also talk of extending the nine months' total to twelve months. In addition, parents can also take up to four months' unpaid leave at any stage, until the child reaches age eight.

Iceland also has exceptionally good health care. The infant mortality rate is essentially the lowest in the world. With a birth rate of almost fourteen births per one thousand people, and a death rate of about half that number, the Icelandic population is growing at a rate of about 1.21 percent per year.

Child-rearing duties fall disproportionately on mothers, in part because fathers generally work very long hours. Since many mothers also work, about 90 percent of children aged one to five years are in daycare.

EDUCATION

The Icelandic educational system is divided into four levels, only one of which is compulsory. They include the preschool level, from twelve months to six years of age; compulsory school, which comprises primary and lower secondary school combined, for children six to sixteen years of age; upper secondary school, for students ages sixteen to twenty; and higher education, for students ages nineteen or twenty and older.

Education is compulsory from the age of six to sixteen. Schooling is free and textbooks are provided by the local government. The standardized curriculum provides a grounding in the various core subjects. Danish is taught from the fourth grade and English from the sixth grade. Swimming is an obligatory part of the curriculum. Children are not divided by abilities at this level of schooling. This encourages a sense of egalitarianism.

Students partake in a range of sports, with handball and soccer being the two most popular. Horseback riding is popular with both boys and girls. Chess and bridge are also popular among students. The easy access to swimming pools heated by geothermal energy makes swimming popular among most young people.

At the end of the ninth grade, a standardized test, along with the school's record of assessment, is used to select what institution a young Icelander

Students work together on a class field trip to the town of Vik in South Iceland.

should go to next. Students may go on to secondary or comprehensive school for four years (ages sixteen to twenty) or to vocational school. Some leave school altogether at sixteen.

Iceland has four public universities: the University of Iceland in Reykjavik, founded in 1911, is the oldest and the largest institution of higher education; the University of Akureyri, Hólar University College, and the Agricultural University of Iceland. Iceland's three private universities are Reykjavik University, the Iceland Academy of the Arts, and Bifröst University. They are all state-funded and tuition is free. About fourteen thousand students attend the University of Iceland every year. Most Icelandic students continue living with their parents during their undergraduate studies, in view of the high price of housing in Reykjavik.

Reykjavik University

WORK FOR YOUTHS

After the age of sixteen, it is common for Icelandic students to hold down a part-time job in addition to continuing their schooling. Jobs such as serving in cafés or helping out in stores are characteristically filled by young people. Other possible jobs include labor-intensive social services, such as looking after the elderly and the disabled. In addition to this part-time work, these students also take temporary jobs in the summer—supervising the younger children employed by the city to tidy up sidewalks or helping to beautify parks, for example.

Much of the money earned by students at this stage is spent on socializing. There are many garage bands playing rock music that have a local following. The major focus of the social scene, however, is downtown Reykjavik on a Friday night. For this occasion, young people dress up in their most fashionable clothes and hit the town to see and be seen, partying into the wee hours of the morning.

The new Harpa Concert Hall and Conference Center in Reykjavik opened in May 2011.

ENTERTAINMENT

When they are not working, Iceland's adults are active cultural consumers. The success of concerts, plays, and art exhibitions in Reykjavik is premised upon a large proportion of the population of the city turning out to see the latest cultural event, and that expectation is generally fulfilled. Icelanders also read widely, eagerly perusing newly published books, not to mention the five national newspapers.

Television is, of course, the easiest option for an evening's entertainment. However, Icelanders vegetate in front of the television far less than people in most other nations, including the United States. Until twenty years ago, television did not broadcast on Thursdays to encourage Icelanders to take part in other social activities.

RELIGION

The dazzling tower of the Hallgrimskirkja Church can be seen from almost everywhere in Reykjavik.

8

WHEN THE NORWEGIAN VIKINGS settled in Iceland, they brought the gods of Norse paganism with them. However, Christianity arrived a couple of centuries later, and Iceland remains a largely Christian country today. About 75 percent of Icelanders are Lutheran. The constitution recognizes the Evangelical Lutheran Church as the state church. However, the constitution guarantees freedom of worship for any faith.

A portion of the taxes Icelanders pay goes to support the activities of the church. Those who do not want to support the church can opt to have their payments support the University of Iceland instead. 73.8 percent of Icelanders belong to the Church of Iceland. A minority identifies with the Seventh-Day Adventists, the Catholic Church, or a rival Lutheran sect. A small group professes pagan beliefs. Immigration in the past decade has also given rise to small Muslim, Jewish, and Buddhist communities.

Despite the large membership in the established church, religion does not play a particularly noticeable part in most people's daily lives. A strikingly high number of people profess belief in such folk traditions as ghosts and trolls.

A 2015 poll of religious attitudes in Iceland made headlines when it found that 0.0 percent of Icelanders under the age of twenty-five believed that God created the world. While the data points to a growing secularism in Icelandic society, some analysts caution that the responses should not be interpreted to mean no young Icelanders believe in God.

NORSE PAGANISM

The ancient pre-Christian religion is unusually well-entrenched in Iceland and has been revived by a small group of modern pagans. Local chieftains acted as pagan priests in early times. Pagans believed in an extensive pantheon of gods and may have also practiced various forms of animism. The gods exist in a parallel world surrounded by such other races as giants and dwarves. Their cosmos is kept together by Yggdrassil, the World Ash Tree—the Old Norse version of the cosmic tree.

Odin is the chief god of Norse mythology. He is the god of poetry, wisdom, and war. He became god of poetry by stealing the mead of poetry from the dwarves. He acquired wisdom by sacrificing his eye at the well of wisdom and by hanging himself on the cosmic tree for three days. Warriors who dedicated themselves to Odin could induce in themselves a war frenzy in which they entered an altered state. In this frenzied state they could feel no pain, which made them very effective as warriors. Such warriors were known as berserkir *(BAIR-zerh-kaihr), from which we get the English word* berserk, *meaning out of control with anger or excitement, or raving.*

Thor (Þor) is the most single-minded of the gods. He lacks the intellectual side of Odin but generally succeeds in what he sets out to achieve through brute force. His

strength is associated with his hammer and is manifested in his creation of thunder. Many Old Icelandic personal names included the word Thor, suggesting that he was worshipped particularly widely in Iceland.

Frey and his sister Freya are important fertility gods. They are responsible for the productivity of crops and the fertility of animals and humans.

Loki is part god, part giant. He is the trickster god, sometimes playing friendly practical jokes, sometimes thoroughly mean ones. Perhaps his worst deed is his responsibility for the death of Baldur.

Baldur is the son of Odin. He is so beloved by everyone and everything that all of creation agrees not to hurt him. Since this was the case, the gods throw things at him at parties, marveling at how nothing ever hurts him. This galls Loki, who searches for any object that has not pledged not to hurt Baldur. He finally finds that the humble mistletoe has not taken part in the vow. He takes a piece of mistletoe, uses his magic to make it into a dart, and gives it to Baldur's blind half-brother, Hodd, to throw at Baldur while the gods are having their fun. Everyone is devastated with grief when the mistletoe pierces Baldur and kills him. Loki is eventually punished for this deed. This is the origin of the tradition of people kissing beneath the mistletoe, making a gesture of peace to atone for its misdeed in killing Baldur.

The Norse gods are not particularly moral. Odin sleeps with many different women. He even cheats in his role of selector of the slain in battle. He sometimes unfairly makes the best warrior lose and die so that he can enjoy his company in Valhalla. Unlike the Greek and Roman gods, the Norse gods were mortal, finally dying at Ragnarok (the doom of the gods) in a pitched battle with their enemies. The fact that the gods lose this final battle may explain some of the traditional bleakness of Old Norse culture. At this stage, Baldur comes back to life and the younger generation of gods takes over.

One of the most famous ghosts is the spirit of Glámur in Grettir's Saga. *Glámur, a strong and antisocial shepherd, is killed on Christmas Eve by a ghost near Vatnsdal and is not buried in sanctified ground. As a result, his spirit takes to haunting the farm, including riding on the housetops. He kills the shepherd who replaces him the next Christmas, and generally terrorizes the farmers and their families. Finally the strong man Grettir, hero of the saga, undertakes to help the farmers by challenging the ghost, Glámur, to a duel. The ghost kills Grettir's horse and Grettir waits for a nighttime encounter with Glámur.*

When about a third of the night has passed, Grettir hears a loud noise. Something is climbing up the building, riding the roof and kicking with its heels until the timber beams crack. This goes on for some time, and then the thing comes down toward the door. The door opens and Grettir sees Glámur's enormously big and ugly head looming in the door. Glámur moves slowly in, and on passing the door stands upright, reaching to the roof. He turns toward the hall, resting his arms on the crossbeam and peering into the room.

Glámur and Grettir then engage in a mighty wrestling match, destroying much of the hall in the process. At first, Grettir tries to prevent Glámur from dragging him outside, then suddenly overpowers him by switching tactics and pushing him out the door.

Glámur falls head over heels out of the house and Grettir falls on top of him. The moon is shining very brightly outside, with light clouds passing over it and hiding it now and again. At the moment when Glámur falls, the moon shines forth, and Glámur turns his eyes up toward it. Grettir himself relates that that sight is the only one that ever made him tremble. With the fatigue, the loss of his horse, and all else that he has endured, when he sees the horrible rolling of Glámur's eyes, Grettir's heart sinks so utterly that he has no strength to draw his sword, but lies there between life and death. Glámur possesses more malignant power than most fiends, for he now speaks this way:

"You have expended much energy, Grettir, in your search for me. Nor is it to be wondered at that you should have little joy thereof. And now I tell you that you shall possess only half the strength and firmness of heart that were decreed to you if you had not striven with me. And this I lay upon you, that these eyes of mine shall be ever before your vision. You will find it hard to live alone, and at last it shall drag you to death."

When the specter finishes speaking, the faintness that had come over Grettir leaves him. He draws his short sword, cuts off Glámur's head, and lays it between his thighs. Thorhall the farmer praises God and thanks Grettir warmly for having laid to rest this unclean spirit. Then they set to work and burn Glámur to cold cinders, bind the ashes in a skin, and bury them in a place far away from the haunts of man or beast.

After this incident, Grettir, the great strong man and outlaw, is afraid to be alone in the dark.

INTERNET LINKS

www.oikoumene.org/en/member-churches/evangelical-lutheran-church-of-iceland
The World Council of Churches page for the Evangelical Lutheran Church of Iceland relates the history of the church.

www.theatlantic.com/international/archive/2013/10/why-so-many-icelanders-still-believe-in-invisible-elves/280783
The *Atlantic* offers a good article about folk beliefs in Iceland.

www.zuistar.is/english.html
The Zuist Church of Iceland website states its objectives in English.

LANGUAGE

A road sign in the fjord of Akureyri warns of ducks crossing.

9

ICELANDIC IS ESSENTIALLY THE language of the people of Western Norway who first settled the island more than one thousand years ago. The difference is that Norwegian changed over the years, as the people came to be ruled by Sweden and Denmark. The language evolved in Norway, but not in Iceland. There, due to the island's isolation, the Old Norse language remained much the same. Some say Icelandic, therefore, is a linguistic form of time travel back to the age of the Vikings.

Icelandic is a distant cousin to the English language. The long ago origins of both languages lie in an old Germanic language shared both by the Angles and Saxons who later migrated to England, and by the predecessors of the Viking Norwegians who later migrated to Iceland. The different languages have, of course, developed in very different ways. Icelandic is a strikingly standardized and conservative language. There are almost no dialectal variants between regions in spoken Icelandic, unlike the vast array of dialects of spoken English.

Modern Icelandic is quite close to Old Icelandic. The Old Icelandic language of the medieval Icelandic sagas is fairly easy for today's Icelanders to read. In contrast, the Old English of *Beowulf*, the epic Anglo-Saxon poem of similar age, is almost indecipherable to modern English readers.

English has changed considerably in the last thousand years. As the Anglo-Saxons suffered conquest by the Normans, rediscovered Greek and Latin culture, and explored the New World, their language was influenced by these encounters. Icelandic, on the other hand, changed little over this time.

The English language accepts words from other languages very readily. Words like "burrito" and "potato" are taken from another language to describe a concept or object new to English. Such borrowings are known as loan words. English also borrows readily from Greek and Latin to explain new concepts, such as "telephone," which is made up of the Greek words for "far" and "sound," or "television," made up from the Greek word for "far" and the Latin word for "seeing."

Icelandic is very resistant to such borrowings. A form of the word "telephone" has been absorbed into most languages (German telefon, *French* téléphone, *Italian* telefono*). The Icelandic word is* sími *(SEE-mi), which is an adaptation of a native word for a length of thread. Likewise, Icelanders resist using the term "computer," which is called* tölva *(TEHL-vah), a blend of the Icelandic words* tala *(TAO-lah), meaning "number," and* völva *(VEHL-vah), meaning "prophetess."*

One standard method of word formation in Icelandic is by combining existing words (such as "birdbath" in English). The resulting compound words can be rather a mouthful. For example, the treasury is called fjármálaráduneyti *(FYAHR-mahl-rah-thoh-NAY-ti; where* fjár *= money,* mál *= matter or affairs,* rád *= plan or authority,* ráduneyti *= a department); an idealist is a* hugsjónamadur *(HOHGS-yoon-nah-MAH-thor; where* hugsun *= thought,* sjón *= vision,* madur *= person); and a rebel is an* uppreisnarmadur *(OHP-prize-nahr-MAH-thor; an uprising person).*

THE ICELANDIC ALPHABET

Icelandic has a number of letters in addition to those in the English alphabet. Þ þ (upper case and lower case) is known as *thorn* (replaced by *th* when Anglicized), represents the sound of the English *th* in a word like "thin." Ð and ð, known as *eð* (Anglicized using the letter *d*) and represents the sound "eth" or "edh."

Vowels have two forms, with and without accents. Icelandic has a differentiated set of long vowels, which are spelled with an accent, as in í. Icelandic also has the vowels ö and æ, which represent the sounds of the vowel in the English words "turn" and "eye."

The letter þ derives from an earlier form of script, known as the runic alphabet, which was used for inscriptions in Old Icelandic. This same script was also occasionally used in Old English for inscriptions and throughout Northern Europe in medieval times.

The letter z is no longer used and was officially removed from the Icelandic alphabet in 1973. Its sound in Icelandic was indistinguishable from the sound of s and the letter was therefore replaced with s.

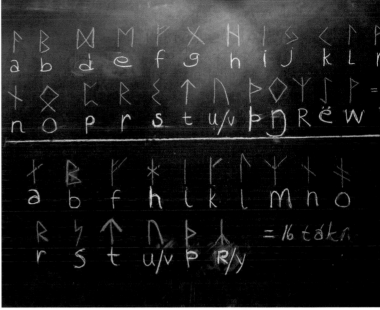

The runic alphabet predates the modern Roman alphabet, but the runic letter Þ (thorn) survives in modern Icelandic.

THE NAMING SYSTEM

Surnames or family names came into English gradually over the course of the last thousand years. The system of naming that evolved is similar in most countries. Iceland, however, retains an older system where everybody has only one name, a first name. For the most part—there are a few exceptions—there are no family names. In order to distinguish individuals with the same name, a patronymic is added after the first name.

Boys and men make their patronymic through the suffix -son, as in Jón Sigurdsson, who would generally be called Jón and whose father was Sigurd. His own son might be called Magnús Jonsson. A woman named Gudrún Erlendsdóttir is called Gudrún in both informal and formal circumstances. Her second name, or patronymic, is simply the name of her father, Erlendur, with the suffix -dóttir, meaning "daughter."

First names are subject to approval by the Icelandic Naming Committee. This entity was established in 1991 to exert legal control over Icelandic names, ensuring that they are compatible with Icelandic grammar and traditions. For example, a name must be spelled only using the Icelandic alphabet, which does not include the letter C. Therefore, a female name such as Christine must be spelled Kristine. Parents may not invent names for their child, or use foreign names, but must use previously approved Icelandic names from a list of 1,853 female and 1,712 male names.

In addition, the law frowns on using a name of the opposite gender. The Personal Names Act of 1996 states, "Girls shall be given women's names, and boys shall be given men's names. A forename may not be such as to cause its bearer embarrassment." Parents who wish to challenge the law may take the case to court, as some have. In 2013, a fifteen-year-old girl named Blær Bjarkardóttir petitioned the court to have her birth name Blær legally recognized. The name had remained approved because it is traditionally considered a male name. However, in this case, young Blær won her case.

On the other hand, in another recent case, the names Duncan and Harriet, given to the Icelandic-born children of a British father and an Icelandic mother, were not initially approved. The siblings had to be listed on official forms, such as passports, as Drengur *("boy") and* Stulka *("girl"). The parents pursued the case through the courts until they won their case. As a result of this case, government officials in Iceland are considering doing away with the naming committee.*

In some cases, a matronymic name is used. Those names are derived from the mother. Gudrún might name her daughter Sigrún Þórsson if the child's father's name is Þór. However, for a variety of reasons, Gudrún might prefer to name the girl Sigrún Gudrúnsdóttir, after herself.

One consequence of this mostly patronymic system is that grandparents are not connected to their grandchildren by name. Magnús Jonsson's son might be called Páll Magnússon, which gives no clue that his grandfather was Jón Sigurdsson. Another consequence is that there is no question of a woman changing her name when she gets married. She keeps her own name.

In the Icelandic telephone directory, everyone is listed and the entries are alphabetized by first name. It is proper to refer to everybody by that name except for two dignitaries, who are addressed by their title: the president and the bishop of Iceland.

A fossil of this patronymic system remains in English family names, as in the names "Johnson" or "Harrison." Clearly, such names make up a small group of family names in English, and those names have been passed down through the generations to the point where no one remembers who the original John or Harry were.

In Iceland, there was a period in the 1940s when Western European-style family names became popular. This explains the name of the famous Icelandic novelist Halldor Laxness, who chose to adopt a place name as his family name. The system of patronymics is currently very strong, however ninety percent of Icelanders use patronymics, and it's no longer legal to switch to family names. It used to be that any foreigner who adopted Icelandic citizenship also had to adopt a suitable patronymic, but that was changed in the 1990s.

INTERNET LINKS

www.fluentin3months.com/icelandic
"Five Curious Facts You Never Knew About Icelandic" is informative and interesting.

www.iceland.is/the-big-picture/people-society/language
This page gives some background of the language, a few common phrases, and links to related topics.

www.omniglot.com/writing/icelandic.htm
Omniglot offers a basic introduction to Icelandic, with audio files and links.

www.standard.co.uk/news/uk/victory-for-the-siblings-named-girl-and-boy-on-passports-a3283546.html
This 2016 British news article covers the story of one family's name battle in Iceland.

ARTS

The modern sculpture *Solfar* ("Sun Voyager") by Icelandic sculptor Jón Gunnar Árnason stands near the sea in Reykjavik.

10

THERE'S A CERTAIN ROMANCE to Iceland—its starkly beautiful landscapes, its isolation in the northern ocean, its mysterious Viking past. This sensibility imbues its arts and culture with a distinctive Nordic richness that begins with the country's famous sagas. A blend of fact and fantasy, these ancient tales of heroes and kings are Iceland's greatest contribution to literature and history.

The vibrancy of this early literature may be connected to the Icelandic environment—long, dark winter nights before the invention of electric lighting gave early Icelanders ample opportunity for storytelling, while Icelandic sheepskin provided parchment on which to write those tales. Whatever the reason, Iceland has one of the most notable literary traditions of the Middle Ages, and the country continues to have a significant literary scene.

MEDIEVAL LITERATURE

Iceland's sagas are a large body of medieval literature that tell the story of Iceland's first settlers. They began as oral history, passed from one generation to another, relating the genealogy, family feuds, and other events of the ninth, tenth, and eleventh centuries. The art of writing

In Reykjavik, a comic theatrical production called "Icelandic Sagas–The Greatest Hits" is performed several nights a week in English and promises to combine all forty sagas into seventy-five minutes of uproarious fun. The city also celebrates the sagas with statues, exhibitions, and museums.

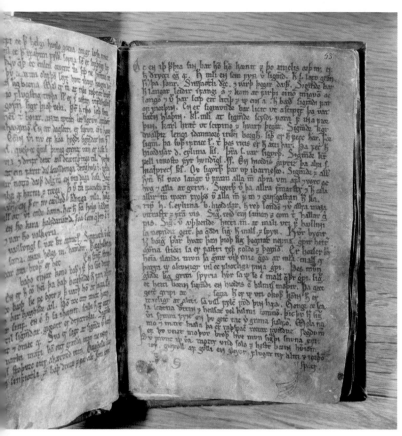

The book called the Codex Regius is the oldest and most important manuscript of the *Elder Edda* verses.

came to the island with Christianity in the eleventh century, and the long, memorized narratives were then recorded. The sagas' narrative prose is unparalleled in other European literature of the time. The sagas are in some ways like novels. They revolve around conflicts between families and questions of honor, glory, loyalty, and revenge, all unfolding in the austere beauty of medieval Iceland.

A striking range of Old Icelandic poetry also survives. There are two poetic traditions. One is derived from an extensive collection of mythological and heroic verse known as the *Elder Edda*. The other is a tradition of extremely complex praise poetry, with many musical effects, such as alliteration, rhyme, half-rhyme, and assonance. This latter kind is known as skaldic verse after the Icelandic name for the poets, skalds, (SKAHLDS) who recited it.

Icelandic skalds were particularly successful at their task of praising kings. Iceland provided court poets throughout much of Europe, chronicling in particular the acts of Norway's kings. These poets acted rather like the journalists of their day, spreading the reputation of deserving (or well-paying) kings and lords in glowing verses.

NJÁLS SAGA

Probably the most famous medieval Icelandic family saga is *Njáls Saga*, also called *The Story of Burnt Njáll*. This gripping thirteenth-century tale tells of the friendship between Njáll, a lawyer and promoter of peace, and Gunnar, a brave and noble hero. The tale relates the bloody, fifty-year feud between

THOR'S HAMMER

Not all the Icelandic mythological poetry is austere and serious. One poem tells of the predicament faced by the gods when the giant Thrym steals Thor's hammer, which is the source of his strength. Thrym demands to be married to Freya before he will return the hammer. Freya absolutely refuses such a suggestion, disdaining the stain on her reputation. The gods meet in council and decide that the only solution is to send Thor in a woman's dress, pretending that he is Freya. Loki accompanies him, dressed as his bridesmaid.

When the two gods get to the wedding feast, Thrym is surprised and perhaps appalled at the vast appetite of his wife-to-be, who devours huge portions with no ladylike manners. Loki explains that "Freya" has been fasting while waiting for the marriage and so is ravenously hungry. Thrym is apparently contented with this answer. Next he lifts up his betrothed's veil to steal a kiss, but leaps back when he sees such fiery red eyes. Loki explains again, claiming that "Freya" has not slept for nights in excited anticipation of the wedding. Finally, Thrym's sister asks what present she is going to get at the wedding. At this point, Thor's hammer is produced to hallow the wedding ceremonies. Thor grabs it and kills all the giants present. Thrym's sister gets a blow from the hammer as her wedding gift.

Gunnar fights off ambushers in this 1897 illustration of Njáls saga.

the families of the two men, who try to keep their friendship intact throughout. As the title suggests, Njáll meets with a fiery—but honorable—end.

As with most of the sagas, the author of Njáll is unknown, though scholars like to speculate. The story survives in about sixty manuscripts and fragments dating from the year 1300 at the earliest, and was probably first composed around 1270. The events themselves take place between 960 and 1020, and reveal a great deal about the earliest culture of the settlers.

Today, the sagas are much loved in Iceland, where parts of them are taught beginning in elementary school. Part folklore, part history, they are seen as the inspiration for *The Lord of the Rings* and *Game of Thrones*, among many other fantasy and Viking dramas.

MODERN LITERATURE

The most famous modern Icelandic writer by far is Halldor Laxness (1902—1998), winner of the Nobel Prize in literature in 1955. He parodied the medieval family sagas in *Gerpla* (1952), in which he satirized the too-ready recourse to violence throughout the ages. Another of his novels, *The Atomic Station*, published in 1948, anticipated the controversy about the US airbase at Keflavík. The novelist was strongly critical of the willingness of Icelandic politicians to give up Iceland's independence. Probably the most famous novel by Halldor Laxness is *Independent People* (1934). Here the novelist promoted the cause of Icelandic independence before the full break from Denmark while not over-glamorizing life in Iceland. He described the gritty and sometimes petty reality of an Icelandic small farmer, while at the same time glorifying that farmer's defiant spirit of independence.

Icelandic literature has continued to thrive since Halldor Laxness. Halldor's novels represent a tradition of social commentary through acute observation of everyday life. Others have written in this tradition, while a non-realist tradition is evident in the modernist works of Thor Vilhjalmsson. His novels have won many literary prizes. Many younger novelists continue to publish interesting works, such as Einar Mar Gudmundsson's *Angels of the Universe*, a novel portraying a man's destructive behavior and his subsequent descent into schizophrenia. This work was awarded the Nordic Council's Literature Award in 1995.

Poetry thrives in modern Iceland and is spurred on not just by the high literacy rate but also by a living tradition of memorizing and reciting poetry. Poets played a significant role in Iceland's struggle for independence. Jonas Hallgrimsson (1807—1845) is one of the most admired poets of modern Iceland. He pioneered a new movement in poetry and literature, which reshaped the language of poetry and prose, opened the Icelanders' eyes to the beauty of their land, and accelerated their determination to achieve political independence. Halldor Laxness calls him the "poet of Icelandic consciousness."

Jon Sigurdsson, the important nineteenth-century independence figure, was a poet. In the twentieth century, Steinn Steinarr was an important modernist poet who wrote in free verse. A group of poets from the 1950s who broke from traditional forms became known as the "atom poets" for their modern approach. The most popular poet of the postwar generation is Hannes Petursson, who turned back to old metrical forms to deal with modern themes. All Icelandic poets show a deep sense of historical tradition by either reacting to the past or revisiting it.

The tomb of Icelandic poet Jonas Hallgrimsson, one of Iceland's most beloved poets, is in the Thingvellir churchyard.

Outlaws is one of three monuments by Einar Jonnson that are installed in various public places in Reykjavik.

Icelandic drama looks back to Matthias Jochumsson's *Útilegumennirnir* (*The Outlaws*, 1862), as the beginning of a tradition blending popular romance with native folktale. The most important modern playwright is Jokull Jakobsson, whose work blends theater of the absurd with realist drama on political themes to search for the meaning of life. Recent work continues the exploration of political and social problems in plays by Kjartan Ragnarsson and others.

VISUAL ARTS

There isn't a very extensive tradition of painting in Iceland. One of the first painters to capture the Icelandic landscape on canvas was Asgrimur Jonsson (1876—1958). He painted the light on the landscape in watercolors influenced by the Impressionists. His home and studio in Reykjavik have become a museum of his art.

Johannes Kjarval (1885—1972) is probably Iceland's most popular painter. He studied briefly in England and was strongly influenced by J.M.W. Turner. His paintings include a range of styles, tending toward the abstract and dreamlike. On his seventieth birthday, a retrospective of his work was viewed by twenty-five thousand people, over an eighth of the population of Iceland at the time. On his death, a museum of his works was established in Reykjavik.

Subsequent artists, such as Thorvaldur Skulason (1906—1984), turned from landscapes to an art engaged with Iceland's urban life or the fishing industry and to more abstract art. Most Icelandic artists receive training abroad. Some have made their home abroad, such as the leading figurative painter Louisa Matthiasdottir (1917—2000) who lived and worked in New York.

Einar Jonsson (1874—1954) was Iceland's first significant sculptor. His early work, *Outlaws*, portrays a scene from *The Saga of Gisli* in realistic style. He subsequently combined this style with a private symbolism. His home is now a museum, where his works are kept on display.

Today, there are a large number of contemporary visual artists in Iceland working in a wide range of styles and mediums.

Sigur Rós performs at London's Academy Brixton in 2013.

MUSIC

Icelandic youths listen to both US and European pop music and a number also play in garage bands. Contemporary pop and indie music has been especially notable in the country. Some of the popular young artists today include the electro pop duo Young Karin and the soft rock duo Andy Svarthol. Olafur Arnalds (b. 1986) is a former hardcore metal band drummer from Mosfellsbær who is now a multi-instrumentalist and producer. In music that ranges from ambient electronic to pop, he mixes stings and piano with loops and beats. His most recent album is *Island Songs* (2016).

One of the best-known groups to achieve international fame is Sigur Rós, a post-rock band from Reykjavik that has been playing since 1994. The group's music has been described as ambient, spacey, progressive, and soundscape. The three- or four-person band features guitarist and vocalist Jon Thor Birgisson, known as "Jonsi." In 2013, the group released its seventh studio album, *Kveikur*.

Classical music came relatively late to Iceland. Icelandic music remained essentially medieval into the nineteenth century. In relatively recent times, the necessary institutions for classical music have developed on a small scale, with the founding of the Reykjavik Conservatory of Music in 1930, the

National Symphony Orchestra in 1950, and a biennial Reykjavik Festival of the Arts since 1970. There are now high quality classical concerts in Reykjavik all summer long.

Movie posters decorate a billboard in Reykjavik.

MOVIES

Around 1980, a fledgling Icelandic movie industry began making movies that gained some international recognition. Many of the earlier movies harkened back to the Saga Age, and movies that feature Vikings are still popular, both in Iceland and abroad.

Icelandic filmmakers are mainly concerned with Icelandic attitudes, history, and subjects of importance for Icelanders, reflecting pride in their land and traditions. But some have combined Icelandic topics with Western filmmaking styles, such as Hrafn Gunnlaugsson's movie, *When the Raven Flies*, which portrays medieval Iceland through the conventions of the spaghetti Western. Thorsteinn Jonsson's *The Atomic Station*, based on the

THE HIGH PRIESTESS OF ART-POP

Internationally, probably the best-known Icelandic singer-songwriter-actress is Björk (b. 1965). The singer, who goes by her first name only, first gained fame in the alternative-rock group The Sugarcubes from 1986 to 1992, but went on to greater reknown as a solo artist.

Björk's musical style has changed and evolved greatly over the years, and music critics find her impossible to categorize. She blends electronica, jazz, rock, classical, and experimental forms in unique ways, and has been described as the "high priestess of art-pop" and other similar appellations. She is also recognized for her sometimes outrageous fashion, and is especially remembered for wearing the famous "swan dress" at the 2001 Academy Awards. The dress looked like a dead swan hung around her neck.

In 2015, Björk released her ninth studio album, Vulnicura, and performed on a world tour, beginning at Carnegie Hall in New York City. In all, she has sold millions of albums, won numerous top music and acting awards, and been active in environmental causes in Iceland. In 2015, the artist-activist was named one of the one hundred most influential people in the world by Time magazine.

novel of the same name by Halldor Laxness, was shown at the Cannes Film Festival in 1984.

In 1992 Fridrik Por Fridriksson's *Children of Nature* was nominated in the Best Foreign Film category at the Academy Awards. That movie remains Iceland's best-known film internationally.

A new generation of film directors have moved beyond the nostalgia for the past that characterized earlier films, and show a far more diverse approach to modern filmmaking. *Jar City* (2006) by Baltasar Kormákur, *Volcano* (2011) by Runar Runarsson, and *Of Horses and Men* (2013) by Benedikt Erlingsson are some notable examples. More recently, the drama *Rams* (2015) was a prize winner at the Cannes Film Festival.

CRAFTS

Icelandic sheep need thick fleece to endure the rigors of the Icelandic winter. The outer layer of coarse wool is naturally waterproof, while the inner layers of fine wool retain warmth close to the skin. The fleece, which is shorn from

A shop in Center Town, Reykjavik, displays iconic Icelandic sweaters for sale.

the sheep in the spring and spun into high-quality wool yarn, forms the basis for the traditional Icelandic handicraft of knitting warm sweaters.

There is a classic design for traditional Icelandic sweaters. The body is generally white or earth-toned, while a geometric pattern at the yoke adds a splash of color and design. Iceland's international airport at Keflavík is a thriving outlet for Icelandic knitwear. Passengers traveling between the United States and Europe have every opportunity to boost the economy of Iceland by buying an Icelandic sweater even during the shortest of layovers.

INTERNET LINKS

www.bfi.org.uk/news-opinion/news-bfi/lists/10-great-icelandic-films
This article explores some of the best Icelandic films.

www.bjork.com
This is the artist Björk's official site in English.

www.iceland.is/arts-culture
This site offers a good look at today's arts and culture scene in Iceland.

olafurarnalds.com
This is the website of the musician Ólafur Arnalds.

sagadb.org
The Icelandic Saga Database has all of the sagas available in a number of languages, including English.

sigur-ros.co.uk
The official site of Sigur Rós lists tour dates, news, photos, and videos.

time.com/3823157/bjork-2015-time-100
This is the "Time 100" listing for Björk.

LEISURE

The Icelandic handball player Robert Gunnarsson, in blue, tries to score against Spanish goalie José Javier Hombrados during a World Championship meet in Germany.

11

COMPARED TO PEOPLE IN OTHER European nations, Icelanders work long hours—an average of forty-seven hours a week for men, and thirty-seven hours a week for women. On top of that, working overtime is quite common. So leisure time is not something many Icelanders have a great deal of. Compared to people in other Nordic countries, Icelanders have significantly less time for leisure and personal care. Nevertheless, like other Nordic folks, Icelanders enjoy the great outdoors.

Given Iceland's terrain and climate, however, outdoor activities can be a challenge. Rainy, windy, cold days are common, even in the summer. This might explain why Icelanders love reading. Some say reading is the national sport! According to a 2013 survey, about 50 percent of Iceland's people read at least eight books a year, and 93 percent read at least one. More remarkable, perhaps, than those impressive statistics, is the claim that one in ten Icelanders will publish a book in their lifetime.

Chess is also a popular pastime. Iceland has more grandmasters of chess per capita than any other country. The Icelandic National Chess Championship is an important contest, as is the Reykjavik Open tournament, which the capital city has hosted since 1964.

"Handball, for us, has become not just a sport, but the core of the national spirit."
—Olafur Ragnar Grimsson, president of Iceland, 1996-2016

SPORTS

Icelanders are great fans of soccer, but outdoor stadiums and playing fields were not realistic venues for Iceland. In recent years, Iceland has built almost 150 state-of-the art all-weather domed playing fields and indoor arenas. Children can now play soccer year-round and many towns sponsor local teams.

The investment paid off. Being such a small country, Icelanders never expected their national soccer team to take on the world powers. The 2016 season, however, proved to be remarkable. The team qualified for the Euro 2016 Football (Soccer) Tournament in Paris—which in itself was amazing, making Iceland the smallest nation ever to qualify for a major soccer tournament. The team then went all the way to the quarterfinals, beating England in round 16, and found itself up against the host team, France. Just as astonishingly, nearly 10 percent of the population of Iceland traveled to Paris to attend the match and cheer for *Strákarnir Okkar* ("Our Boys"). Although

Antoine Griezmann of France (*left*) takes command of the ball from Iceland's Kolbeinn Sigthorsson in a match at the UEFA (European Football) Euro 2016.

Iceland ultimately lost to France 5—2, the team garnered the respect and admiration of soccer fans the world over, and created joyful hysteria back home.

After soccer, handball is the most popular year-round game, since it is played on indoor courts. Iceland ranks among the top nations in the world at this fast-paced game. At the 2008 Summer Olympics in Beijing, Iceland's handball team brought home the silver medal, making Iceland the smallest country ever to medal in an Olympic team sport. More than 80 percent of Icelanders watched the final match on television that summer, and even though the team ultimately lost the gold to France, Iceland's President Olafur Ragnar Grimsson awarded the team members the Knight's Cross, one of the highest honors in the country.

Boxing is banned in Iceland, but there is a traditional form of Icelandic wrestling known as *glíma* (GLEE-mah), which has been practiced since the early days of settlement in Iceland. Similar in many ways to Japanese sumo wrestling, glíma wrestlers wear harnesses on their thighs and hips which their opponent grabs in an attempt to throw them to the ground.

Icelanders do well in international contests in track and in sports relying on strength. Vala Flosadóttir won the 2000 Olympic bronze medal for pole vaulting.

OUTDOOR ACTIVITIES

Horseback riding was the usual means of land transportation throughout Iceland for centuries. It remains a significant pastime today, offering the opportunity to explore the beauty of the remote parts of the country.

Swimming is a popular activity. Small communities have outdoor pools where the water is heated by geothermal energy. As swimming is a compulsory part of the school curriculum, all Icelanders can swim. Many public pools also include a hot tub or jacuzzi of hot water for relaxing in. Public pools, called *sundlaugs*, serve as communal gathering places in many towns. Families, children, old folks, and teens like to hang out, socialize, or just relax in the water—summer and winter alike. In fact, many people say the best time to enjoy the heated outdoor water is on the coldest of days.

Hiking is a favorite activity for both Icelanders and tourists as this enables them to take in the starkly beautiful scenery of the coast and interior. Fishing for salmon and trout is also a popular activity, although fishing licenses can be very expensive. Hunting is popular, particularly of ptarmigan in the fall.

Skiing is a favorite sport and there are some good ski resorts throughout Iceland. Bláfjöll, Iceland's largest ski resort, is located just thirty minutes away from Reykjavik. Cross-country skiing is a popular alternative to hiking in winter. Locals and tourists also take advantage of the outdoor splendors by snowmobiling, ice-climbing, and trekking over glaciers.

Iceland's environment is not ideal for golf due to the lack of smooth areas of earth, the strong winds, and the unpredictable weather. Nevertheless, golf is played at a number of courses throughout Iceland. There is an international tournament called the Arctic Open, which takes advantage of the midnight sun during the summer at Akureyri in the north. In late June a thirty-six-hole international match is held, with tee-off at midnight and play continuing until the early hours of the morning.

FRIDAY NIGHT

On the weekend in Reykjavik, and especially on Friday nights, young people head out for a night on the town. The crowd in their twenties—twenty is the legal drinking age—may spend the evening in a bar or at a club. Those under twenty years old also hit the town and are generally more visible in their celebrations. The festivities usually go on very late.

Friday night gives Icelandic youths an opportunity to dress up in the latest fashions. Typically, a group of friends will congregate at someone's house in the evening for some conversation before heading downtown. Around midnight, the group goes to the bars or clubs downtown, meet other friends, and generally see what is happening and be seen. It is unfashionable to turn up before midnight. Those with access to cars—seventeen is the minimum age for getting a license—cruise in a fashion-conscious traffic jam known as *runtur*, a circuit of the downtown streets that is the place to be on a Friday night.

ICELANDIC HORSES

Icelandic horses are small but sturdy beasts. They are a distinctive breed, descended from horses brought over by the early settlers. No horses have been imported into Iceland for the last eight hundred years, so that the stock has evolved to best suit local conditions. The resulting horses are remarkably sure-footed at covering the unstable and lava-strewn terrain of the Icelandic countryside.

Icelandic horses are unique for having a distinctive fifth gait. The four gaits usual to all horses are the walk, trot, canter, and gallop. Icelandic horses have a gait between the trot and canter, known as the tölt (tehlt), which is faster than a trot but smoother than a canter, with the rider staying secure in the saddle. This makes it ideal for covering long distances at a comfortable pace.

INTERNET LINKS

www.nytimes.com/2016/04/24/magazine/icelands-water-cure.html?_r=0
Iceland's outdoor heated pool culture is explored and explained.

www.nytimes.com/2016/07/03/sports/soccer/euro-iceland-france.html
This engaging article looks at the popularity of Iceland's soccer team in 2016.

www.visiticeland.com/things-to-do/activities/the-icelandic-horse
This site provides an article with photos about the Icelandic horse.

FESTIVALS

People gather for the 2015 lighting ceremony of the Oslo Christmas Tree in the center of Reykjavik.

WITH ICELAND'S LONG DARK winter, imagine how dreary life would be without holidays and festivals! Happily, there are many special occasions and events to brighten the Icelandic year. Holidays reflect the culture's Viking heritage, Christian religion, national history, and Nordic folklore.

One of the more offbeat celebrations, for those who are twenty years or older, is Bjordagur, or Beer Day, on March 1, which marks the day in 1989 that ended a seventy-four year ban on beer in Iceland. There is no official way to observe Bjordagur, but not surprisingly, the pubs and bars tend to be busy that day. Jonsmessa (Saint John's Day), or Midsummer Night, on June 24, finds some folks rolling naked in the dew-coated grass—it's said to be an especially healing endeavour on that night. According to folklore, it's a good time to make a wish, for it will surely come true. Also on that magical night, cows speak in human languages, seals shed their skins and become humans, and elves are up to mischief.

Icelanders also celebrate with a large number of music and arts fests, particularly during the summer when people can congregate outdoors. For example, in the town of Hafnarfjordur, the annual Viking Festival takes place in June. Costumed celebrants can watch—or take part in—simulated battles, axe throwing and archery contests, and mas-wrestling competitions. There are storytellers, street performers, Viking bands, and crafts markets.

12

Every year, the city of Oslo, Norway, donates a Christmas tree to Reykjavik. The Oslo Tree, as it's called, is placed in Austurvöllur Square and lit for the first time in late November at a ceremony typically attended by more than one thousand people.

CALENDAR OF FESTIVALS

Date	Festival
January 1	New Year's Day
January 6	Epiphany, last day of Christmas season
Late January (first sighting of sun)	Sun Coffee
January/February (varies)	Thorrablot
March (seven weeks before Easter)	Bolludagur, Sprengidagur, Oskudagur
April (varies)	Easter
Third Thursday in April	First day of summer
First Sunday in May	Seamen's Day
June 17	Independence Day
June 21	Midsummer Night
First weekend of August	Verslunarmannahelgi
September	Rettir
December 24–25	Christmas
December 31	New Year's Eve

NEW YEAR'S EVE

New Year's Eve is celebrated in Reykjavik with a vast and spectacular fireworks display at midnight. Many communities celebrate with gatherings around large bonfires.

SUN COFFEE

Communities surrounded by mountains, such as Isafjordur in the western fjords, lose all sight of the sun for an extended time in winter, even on days that are not overcast. In such communities, there is a celebration of the first day on which the sun becomes visible over the surrounding mountains at a festival called Sólarkaffi ("Sun Coffee"). People celebrate the first sighting of the sun with a special serving of coffee and fancy cakes.

THORRABLOT

Þorrablót, (THOR-a-ploat), spelled Thorrablot in English, is a welcoming of the traditional month of Þorri (Thorri), which begins midwinter in January or February. Days are still very dark at this time, so this festival provides a welcome opportunity to party. Traditional food is eaten on this day. One of the most traditional dishes—probably only for adults—is *hákarl* (HAO-kahl), shark meat that has been softened by leaving it to rot for three to six months. It is washed down with *brennivín* (BREN-i-vin), an

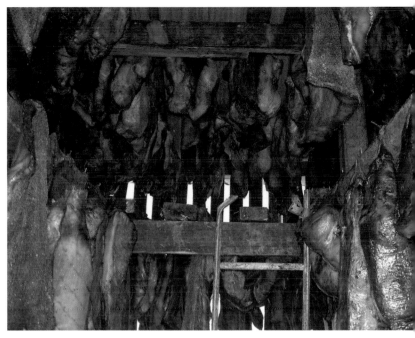

Hunks of hákarl hang in preparation for Thorrablot.

Icelandic form of vodka made from distilled potatoes flavored with angelica. This firewater has the nickname "black death," due to its strong alcoholic kick. This seems to make the rotten shark meat more palatable.

Another traditional food to be eaten on Thorrablot is *svid* (SVEETH). This is a dish that makes full use of the sheep that are such an important part of Icelandic farming. Svid is the head of a sheep, singed to remove the wool, then boiled. It is served complete with the tongue and eyes! Again, appropriately enough, it is washed down with brennivin.

BEGINNING OF LENT

Ash Wednesday and the two days before it are enjoyable celebrations for Icelandic children. Monday is *Bolludagur* (BOH-tloo-DAH-gor), named after the *bollur* (BOH-tlor) that mothers bake for this day. These are tasty eclairs filled with cream and covered in chocolate. By tradition, children are given a little stick on this day. It is their holiday task to catch their parents unguarded so that they can whip them on the rump with the stick. For each successful attack, a child receives one of the delicious bollur.

The next day, Shrove Tuesday, is Sprengidagur (SPREN-gi-DAH-gor), which means "Bursting Day." This is a day of feasting on the traditional meal of *saltkjöt* (SALT-kioht)—salted mutton—with mashed potatoes and green beans.

The next day is Ash Wednesday, Öskudagur (EHSK-oo-DAH-gor). On this day, children make little pouches with fabric and run after unsuspecting grown-ups, trying to surreptitiously attach as many pouches as possible to their backs. In the past, these pouches would have been full of ashes. These days, children also dress up in costumes and go trick-or-treating to gather candies, a tradition similar to Halloween in the United States.

EASTER

Easter is celebrated with Easter eggs and perhaps a trip to church, much as in the United States. It is the center of a lengthy break in the school calendar. Families often go to their country houses at this time.

OTHER FESTIVALS

FIRST DAY OF SUMMER *Sumardagurinn fyrsti*, "the first day of summer" is celebrated on the third Thursday in April, even though it's not the summer solstice or the start of the summer season according to the modern Western calendar. (In olden times, people throughout Europe divided the year into two seasons, summer and winter. The beginning of warm weather for planting was considered the beginning of summer. This explains why the summer solstice in June—the first day of summer according to the Western calendar—is still sometimes called midsummer.) There are parades on this day and candy for the children. Despite the name of the holiday, the weather is rarely summerlike and it often rains.

SEAMEN'S DAY Icelanders celebrate their traditional link with the sea on the first Sunday in June. Sjómannadagur ("Seamen's Day") celebrates the fishermen and other workers of the sea, who make such an important contribution to the Icelandic economy. There are parades in communities

Street performers add to the festivities on Independence Day in Reykjavik.

close to the sea, while ships hold an open day in port so that landlubbers can get a taste of life on the ocean.

INDEPENDENCE DAY June 17 is the day of a big parade in celebration of the nation's declaration of independence in 1944. On this day there is street theater and music in Reykjavik and daylong festivities in a carnival atmosphere. Everybody turns up to watch the parade and takes part in the festivities.

VERSLUNARMANNAHELGI Also known as businessperson's weekend, this is a long weekend break on the first weekend in August. On this occasion, Icelanders traditionally take to the countryside and go camping. Young people gather for their own weekend festivals, which take advantage of the long days of light. Bands perform nonstop, while Icelandic youths party and avoid sleeping until they collapse in exhaustion.

RÉTTIR In September in rural areas, it is necessary to gather the sheep, which have roamed freely during the summer. They are rounded up into large sheep pens so that they can be sorted and claimed by their owners, who maintain them through the winter. This gathering is also the occasion for a rural festival, with dancing, eating, and drinking going on in the evenings.

THE CHRISTMAS SEASON

In Iceland, Jól (Yule, or Christmas) is a serious day for religious celebration and for spending time with the family. Christmas festivities peak on Christmas Eve. This is the day when Icelanders exchange presents and eat the traditional Christmas dinner.

Laufabrauð ("Leaf Bread") is a deep-fried thin flatbread with designs cut into it. Preparing and cutting the laufabraud in the weeks before the holiday is a beloved family tradition, much like decorating Christmas cookies. The main course includes *hangikjöt* (HANG-i-KYOHT), a traditional form of smoked lamb, with boiled potatoes and green beans. This is preceded by a large bowl of rice pudding into which a single almond has been mixed. Whoever gets the portion with the almond receives a special present. The day before Christmas Eve also has its traditional meal, featuring the skate fish.

For children, Christmas Eve is preceded by thirteen days that are marked by the arrival of the magical *Jólasveinarnir*, or "Yule Lads." These thirteen white-bearded troll brothers are the children of Gryla, a mean troll woman who likes to eat disobedient children. Icelandic mothers evoke the threat of Gryla to encourage their children to be good. Gryla's sons are harmless but mischievous, as is suggested by their names, such as Candle-Beggar, Bowl-Licker, and Door-Slammer. Each night leading up to Christmas, children leave a shoe by a window. They arise the next morning to find a little gift in their shoe from a Jólasveinn, one of the Yule Lads. If a child has been naughty, however, he or she might find a rotten potato instead. The holiday season then extends for another thirteen days after Christmas as the lads leave one at a time. On the final day of the holiday season, January 6, people celebrate Þrettándinn ("Epiphany") with bonfires and dances.

Four of Icleand's thirteen Yule Lads roam the countryside during the dark days of the Christmas holiday season.

INTERNET LINKS

fjorukrain.is/en
The Fjörukráin ("Viking Village") website includes information and photos of the annual Viking Festival.

www.iceland.is/the-big-picture/people-society/traditions
The traditional Icelandic holidays are explained on this site.

www.roughguides.com/destinations/europe/iceland/festivals
This travel site includes a page about festivals and holidays.

www.thjodminjasafn.is/english/for-visitors/christmas/christmas-traditions
The National Museum of Iceland site traces the history of the country's Christmas traditions.

FOOD

An Icelandic hot dog, with its specific sauces and toppings, is a favorite food.

13

BASED ON ICELAND'S LOCATION AS a small island in the North Atlantic, far from any mainland, it should be no surprise that fish became an essential food for the people who lived there in days of yore. With its northern climate, short growing season, and rocky terrain, not many fruits, vegetables, or grains could be farmed successfully, though a hardy breed of sheep from Norway thrived. The traditional Icelandic diet, therefore, consisted largely of fish, potatoes, and lamb.

Today, the diet of Icelanders is far more varied because the people no longer have to depend completely on their own resources. Most fresh fruits and vegetables are imported, along with any other sort of food they might desire. Nevertheless, the old way of eating remains a part of the Icelandic heritage, and fish, potatoes, and lamb still play a large part in the diet.

EVERYDAY DISHES

Fish is the mainstay of Icelandic cooking. A typical Icelandic dinner is boiled cod or haddock with boiled potatoes and green beans, plus a

Icelanders adore hot dogs, or *pylsur*. Though they look like American hot dogs, their flavor is a bit different because they are made with lamb, with some pork and beef mixed in. Many customers order their frank "*með öllu*," ("with the works")–ketchup, sweet brown mustard, raw onions, fried onions, and remoulade (a mayonnaise-relish sauce).

A plate of
hardfiskur with
blackened rye
bread and butter is
a common snack.

butter sauce. Other fish staples include salmon, herring, perch, sole, plaice, or halibut.

Fish finds a place at the lunch table, too, either smoked or pickled to be eaten on rye bread. *Harðfiskur*, or dried fish also serves as a snack or portable meal. Dehydrated haddock fillets are sold throughout Iceland—one tears off a strip with the teeth and then chews thoroughly. Alternatively, a strip of dried fish can be eaten with butter. Dried fish is also made into crispy chips that look like potato chips and eaten the same way.

The other staple of Icelandic meals is lamb or mutton. *Hangikjöt*, literally hung-lamb, is lamb that has been hung to be smoke-cured. It is a traditional element of the Christmas meal but is also popular at other times. It might be served with boiled potatoes and pickled cabbage. *Saltkjöt* (SALT-kyoht) is salt-mutton, another way of preserving lamb. It is often served with mashed potatoes and green beans.

Vegetables are not particularly common or cooked in particularly imaginative ways. Some vegetables and fruit are locally produced in greenhouses heated by geothermal energy. Otherwise, all vegetables are imported, which makes them expensive.

Both lunch and dinner often feature Icelandic rye bread, which comes in many different forms. There is also a form of rye pancake that is popular.

TRADITIONAL FOODS

Many of Iceland's traditional foods seem exotic or even distasteful to the modern generation as well as to foreigners. However, these particular foods developed from an isolated, harsh, and barely sustainable way of life. In other words, Icelanders in earlier centuries would have starved to death if they had not been willing to eat every part of an animal, and if they hadn't been able to preserve fish and meats in ways that many modern eaters consider revolting. Today, many of the most distinctive traditional dishes retain an association with specific holidays, particularly Thorrablot.

For example, offal from a sheep is minced together with its blood and cooked in the sheep's stomach to make *slátur* (SLAO-tor, meaning

Some tourists who are brave enough to try sviđ report that it tastes better than it looks.

Icelanders love their skyr *(skeer) and have been making it for more than one thousand years. Skyr is a dairy product that resembles Greek yogurt, but is thicker and less tangy. Like yogurt, skyr is made with active cultures of certain bacteria, but technically skyr is a soft cheese. In Iceland, skyr is made from the milk of Icelandic cattle, the only breed of cow in the country. Traditionalists claim that only this milk gives skyr its proper flavor, though others insist it's the specific Icelandic bacterial culture used in the fermentation process. Purists say that modern methods churn out an inferior skyr and that only making it by hand produces the real deal "the way it used to be."*

Skyr came to Iceland from Norway about 1,200 years ago with the Vikings and, in time, became one of Iceland's iconic foods. It's even mentioned in several of the medieval Icelandic sagas. In recent years, the pleasures of the creamy, protein-rich treat have been discovered by the rest of the world. Riding the coattails of the Greek yogurt craze, skyr has become popular in Europe and North America. The Icelandic cattle cannot produce enough milk to keep up with demand, so other breeds are now being used outside Iceland to produce skyr abroad.

A worker makes a batch of Icelandic skyr.

Skyr is sold in much the same way as yogurt is, in plain or flavored varieties. In Iceland, it is essential in a dish called hræringur, *a mixture of skyr and cooked cereal which can be sweetened with fruit for breakfast.*

HRÆRINGUR (MORGUNMATUR, OR "MORNING PORRIDGE")

½ cup (50 grams) oat flakes
1 cup (200 milliliters) water
1 pinch of salt
8 ounces (240 g) plain skyr
2 tablespoons (28 g) honey
4 tablespoons (60 g) fresh blueberries

Directions

*In a small saucepan, bring the water to
a boil. Add salt and oat flakes, lower the
heat and let it simmer for about 10 minutes until the flakes are soft. Let the oats cool for a
short while, then stir in skyr and honey. Top with fresh blueberries. Serves two.*

"slaughter"), a kind of blood-pudding sausage. Another delicacy makes use of pickled ram's testicles. *Svið* (SVEETH), a boiled sheep's head, is still quite common. The brains are removed, but the eyes and tongue are considered delicacies, at least by some people.

Whale meat is cooked like a steak or eaten raw like sushi. Minke whale, which is not endangered, is the only type that finds its way onto the menu these days. In the past, however, strips of whale blubber were cured by hanging them under a bridge for months until they turn black, at which point they could be eaten. Blubber may have once been an important part of the Icelandic diet, but few people eat it today. Interestingly, most whale meat is served in restaurants and consumed by tourists in the mistaken idea that they are eating in the typical Icelandic style. Icelanders themselves hardly ever eat whale.

Hákarl is shark meat that has been buried for three to six months to allow it to ferment, or putrefy. This process makes the meat edible, which in its fresh form, it is not. The fermented shark meat smells terribly ripe. It is eaten raw

The posters in the windows at a Subway restaurant in Reykjavik say "Love Spinach" and "Love Avocado," for some of its sandwich toppings.

in small chunks washed down with *brennivín*, a potent liquor made from fermented potatoes and caraway, at Thorrablot.

Another local delicacy is *lundi*, which is puffin. These little birds are caught in nets, especially on the Westmann Islands, as a source of food. They can be broiled and reportedly taste something like calf's liver.

FAST FOODS AND COFFEE BREAKS

Fast foods such as hot dogs and hamburgers are steadily rising in popularity in Iceland. It is no longer unusual to find an Icelander eating a hot dog with a cola drink in hand. Icelanders are avid consumers of Coca Cola. In fact, Iceland reportedly consumes the most Coca Cola, per capita, in the world!

In Reykjavik, there are numerous fast food outlets. Although there are some American franchises in Iceland—Subway, Domino's, T.G.I. Friday's—there aren't many, and there are no McDonald's or Starbucks. There are, however, plenty of hamburger places and pizza restaurants. And coffee is much loved throughout Iceland. It is practically the only beverage that is readily available throughout Iceland at low cost. Icelanders drink coffee at breakfast, after meals, and with a light snack or cake in midafternoon.

ALCOHOLIC DRINKS

Iceland, like the United States, opted for prohibition of all alcoholic beverages in the early part of the twentieth century. In Iceland, the move satisfied a Lutheran temperance lobby and made a political statement, since the revenue from tax on alcohol went to Denmark. Wine was legalized in 1921, and in 1935 a national referendum voted to legalize spirits. Beer, however, remained illegal until 1989.

The ban on beer was finally lifted because it had become moot. The original reasoning argued that if young people could not drink beer, they would not be attracted by stronger drinks, which in any case would be too expensive for them. In the absence of beer, they would stay untainted by alcohol. Such reasoning was thoroughly disproved by the traditions of Friday night in Reykjavik. Indeed, some bars discovered a loophole that allowed them to add a shot of spirits to a glass of nonalcoholic beer, which made a beverage as alcoholic as beer (but worse-tasting).

Another anomaly of the old system was that Icelanders arriving from abroad were allowed to import a quota of beer. The result was that on the arrival of every flight, Icelanders stopped at the duty-free shop to buy their legal crate of imported beer and then carried their luggage and beverages back to Reykjavik.

On March 1, 1989, known as Beer Day, a vote in the Althing made alcoholic beer once again legal in Iceland. An Icelandic brewing company now brews its own beer as well as foreign beers under license. The cost of beer is strikingly high compared with other countries. This, however, does not seem to discourage its consumption, particularly on the weekends in Reykjavik.

Iceland's distinctive spirit is brennivín, or "burning-wine." This is a type of vodka made from distilled potatoes and flavored with caraway. Its nickname is "black death," which suggests the perils of drinking too much of this strong spirit. Brennivín features in the traditional feasting of Thorrablot. It is also considered an antidote to the cold bleak weather, particularly in the interior. Thus, coffee spiked with brennivín is called "mountain coffee," the kind of coffee that keeps the farmers who have to work in the mountains warm on chilly days.

A connoisseur holds a Kaldi beer up to the light at the Bruggsmidjan Brewery in Arskogsstrond.

KITCHENS AND MARKETS

Icelandic kitchens, like Icelandic homes in general, tend to be very up-to-date and well-equipped. Microwave ovens are commonplace. Kitchens are kept very clean.

Foodstuffs are bought by Icelanders in supermarkets, which are just like small supermarkets in the United States or Europe, but much more expensive. The only exceptions to the high cost of food are certain local products, most notably caviar and dried fish, which are both quite cheap. There is a far greater variety of fish in most Icelandic supermarkets than in Europe or the United States. Considerable care is taken to keep the fish, which is usually quite a recent catch, as fresh as possible.

A Kronan supermarket in Selfoss, Iceland.

Feasting is an important part of many festivals. Extended families gather for such traditional meals as Christmas and Easter. The festival of Thorrablot calls for the inclusion of both family and friends in the celebration.

EATING OUT

Dining out is not much of a tradition for Icelanders although there are quite a few fast-food restaurants around. Reykjavik has a range of international restaurants, although strongly spiced or hot dishes are generally toned down to satisfy local tastes.

There are numerous street kiosks throughout Reykjavik for picking up a quick snack on the go. These serve up French fries, pizza, sausages, and soft drinks, all relatively cheaply. It is also possible to get an economical plate of fish and chips.

There is much more of a traditional café and bar scene. It is easy to get light meals in Reykjavik's cafés. Such meals include open-topped sandwiches, stuffed pancake dishes, or a buffet of cold cuts, known as a smorgasbord, as well as pastries, cakes, and coffee. These cafés are generally pleasant places for sitting around. Bars also serve light meals. Indeed, many cafés by day are bars by night.

INTERNET LINKS

aof.revues.org/7088
This interview in *Anthropology of Food* takes a historical and nutritional look at the Icelandic diet.

www.roughguides.com/destinations/europe/iceland/food-drink
This travel site gives an overview of food and drink in Iceland.

www.saveur.com/gallery/iceland-christmas-recipes
Saveur offers "Ten Recipes for an Iceland-inspired Christmas."

www.seriouseats.com/2012/04/guide-to-food-iceland-fish-whale-skyr-hot-dogs.html
This amusing introduction to Icelandic food has a link to a slideshow gallery.

www.foodandwine.com/articles/should-you-eat-like-an-icelander
This article links Icelanders health and happiness to their diet.

KAKÓSÚPA (ICELANDIC COCOA SOUP)

This sweet soup is traditionally served as a main course.

3 tablespoons (45 g) cocoa powder
3 tablespoons (45 g) sugar
½ teaspoon cinnamon
2 cups (475 mL) water
3 cups (700 mL) milk
1 tablespoon (14 g) potato starch or cornstarch
salt, to taste
heavy cream, crumbled zwieback biscuits

Mix the cocoa powder, sugar, and cinnamon in a saucepan. Add the water gradually and whisk until smooth. Bring to boil and simmer for 5 minutes.

Add the milk, reheat to boiling point, and simmer for 2 to 3 minutes.

Mix the potato starch or cornstarch with a little cold water, stir into the soup. Cook over low heat, stirring, until it has thickened. Remove from heat.

Salt to taste. Garnish with a drizzle of heavy cream and a sprinkle of crumbled zwieback if you wish.

PLOKKFISKUR (ICELANDIC FISH PIE)

This very traditional Icelandic dish translates as "mashed fish" but is often called a fish pie, even though there is no crust.

1 ¼ pounds (560 g) cod, halibut, or haddock, skinned and boned
1 ¼ lb (560 g) potatoes, boiled and peeled
1 white onion, finely chopped
1 ½ cups (350 mL) milk
4 tablespoons (60 g) butter
3 tablespoons (45 g) flour
salt and pepper
2 tablespoons (28 g) fresh, snipped chives

Break up the fish into large flakes. Cut potatoes into pieces about the same size as the fish chunks. Slowly heat the milk in a small saucepan almost to a boiling point.

While the milk is heating, melt the butter in a large saucepan. Add the onions and sauté over medium heat until soft. Do not allow the onions to brown.

Sprinkle flour over the onion, stir well, making sure all the flour is coated with butter. Cook for 1 to 2 minutes. Gradually add warmed milk, stirring continuously. Simmer for 3 to 4 minutes, stirring often, until thickened.

Add the flaked fish and potatoes and stir gently. Season liberally with salt and pepper. Cook over a low heat until heated through.

Serve, and sprinkle each serving with chives. Serve with dark rye bread and butter.

ARCTIC OCEAN

N

A **B** **C** **D**

1

Arctic Circle

Denmark Strait

Grímsey

Dyrafjördur

Drangajökull

Axarfjördur

Eyjafjördur

Skjálfandi

2

Ísafjördur

Húna-flói

Skagafjördur

Siglufjördur

Húsavík

Vopnafjördur

Arnafjördur

Gláma

Höfdakaupstadur

Saudarkrókur

Akureyri

Mývatn

Herdubreid

Jökulsá á Fjöllum

Seudhisfjördur

Patreksfjördur

Héradsvötn

Odádáraun

Jökulsá á Brú

Lagarfljöt

Neskaupstadur

Breidha-fjördur

Blanda

Askja

Trölladyngja

Snæfell

Reydarfjördur

Valthjófsstadur

Snæfellsjökull

Hofsjökull

Vatnajökull

3

Faxaflói

Langjökull

Thórsá

Thórisvatn

Akranes

Thingvellir

Geysir

Gullfoss

REYKJAVÍK

Thingvallavatn

Kópavogur

Hvítá

Hekla

Oræfajökull
(6,952 ft / 2,119 m)

Keflavík

Hafnarfjördur

Torfajökull

Myrdals-jökull

Eyjafjalla

WESTMANN
ISLANDS

Heimaey

Surtsey

4

ATLANTIC OCEAN

● Capital city
• Major town
▲ Mountain Peak

Feet	Meters
Ice cap	Ice cap
9,900	3,000
6,600	2,000
3,300	1,000
1,650	500
660	200
0	0

MAP OF ICELAND

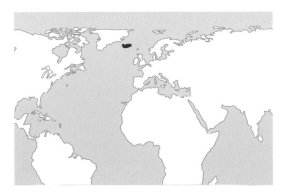

ECONOMIC ICELAND

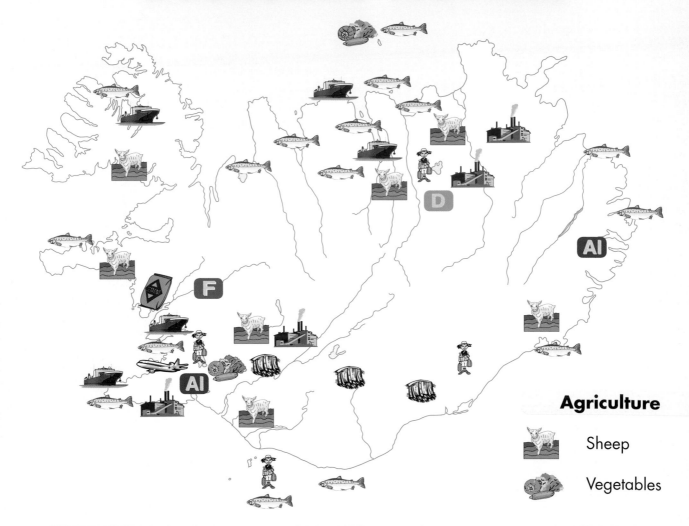

Agriculture

🐑 Sheep

🥦 Vegetables

Natural Resources

D Diatomite

🐟 Fishing

🏭 Geothermal power

⚡ Hydroelectricity

Manufacturing

Al Aluminium smelting

📦 Cement

F Ferrosilicon plant

Services

✈️ Airport

🚢 Port

🧳 Tourism

ABOUT THE ECONOMY

OVERVIEW

The economy depends heavily on the fishing industry, but in the last decade has diversified into the manufacturing and services industries, particularly software production and biotechnology. Tourism has become the main pillar of Icelandic economic growth. The country suffered a collapse of the banking sector in 2008, but following government intervention, it has mostly rebounded from the crisis. Iceland's healthy economy helps its people enjoy a low unemployment rate and a high standard of living.

GROSS DOMESTIC PRODUCT

$15.15 billion (2015 estimate)

TOTAL AREA

Total: 39,768 square miles (103,000 sq km)
Land: 38,707 sq miles (100,250 sq km);
Water: 1,064 sq miles (2,757 sq km)

LAND USE

agricultural land: 18.7 percent
forest: 0.3 percent
other: 81 percent (2011)

NATURAL RESOURCES

Fish, hydropower, geothermal power, diatomite

CURRENCY

Icelandic krona (ISK)
Notes: 5,000; 2,000; 1,000; 500 kronur
Coins: 100, 50, 10, 5, 1 krona
1 USD = 118.290 ISK (August 2016)

INFLATION RATE

1.6 percent (2015)

AGRICULTURAL PRODUCTS

Potatoes, carrots, green vegetables; mutton, chicken, pork, beef, dairy; fish

INDUSTRIES

tourism, fish processing; aluminum smelting, ferrosilicon production; geothermal power, hydropower, tourism

MAJOR EXPORTS

fish and fish products, aluminum, animal products, ferrosilicon, diatomite (2010)

MAJOR IMPORTS

machinery and equipment, petroleum products, foodstuffs, textiles

TRADE PARTNERS

Netherlands, Spain, United Kingdom, Germany, France, United States, Norway, Denmark, China, Brazil

WORKFORCE

190,500 (2015)

UNEMPLOYMENT RATE

3.8 percent (2015)

CULTURAL ICELAND

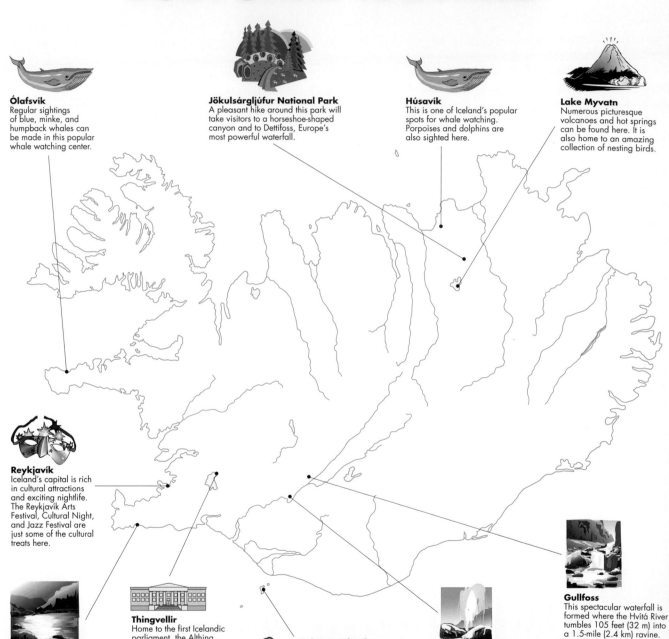

Ólafsvík
Regular sightings of blue, minke, and humpback whales can be made in this popular whale watching center.

Jökulsárgljúfur National Park
A pleasant hike around this park will take visitors to a horseshoe-shaped canyon and to Dettifoss, Europe's most powerful waterfall.

Húsavík
This is one of Iceland's popular spots for whale watching. Porpoises and dolphins are also sighted here.

Lake Myvatn
Numerous picturesque volcanoes and hot springs can be found here. It is also home to an amazing collection of nesting birds.

Reykjavik
Iceland's capital is rich in cultural attractions and exciting nightlife. The Reykjavík Arts Festival, Cultural Night, and Jazz Festival are just some of the cultural treats here.

Thingvellir
Home to the first Icelandic parliament, the Althing.

Blue Lagoon
Bathing in this mineral-rich, geothermally heated pool is said to be excellent for curing skin problems.

Heimaey Island
At the Hæna, Kafhellir, and Hani cliffs reside the world's largest puffin colonies. Watch puffin chicks take flight from these cliffs every August.

Geysir
Great Geyser used to spout regularly to a height of 200 feet (60 m) but is now rather quiet. Strokkur, which is nearby, erupts every few minutes to a height of up to 100 feet (30 m).

Gullfoss
This spectacular waterfall is formed where the Hvítá River tumbles 105 feet (32 m) into a 1.5-mile (2.4 km) ravine.

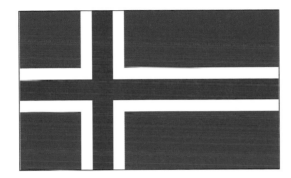

OFFICIAL NAME
Republic of Iceland (Lydveldidh Island)

FLAG DESCRIPTION
Blue with a red cross outlined in white extending to the edges of the flag; the vertical part of the cross is shifted to the hoist side in the style of the Dannebrog (Danish flag)

CAPITAL
Reykjavik

POPULATION
331,918 (July 2015)

ETHNIC GROUPS
Homogenous mixture of descendants of Norse and Celts 94 percent, population of foreign origin 6 percent

RELIGIOUS GROUPS
Evangelical Lutheran Church of Iceland (official), 73.8 percent; Roman Catholic, 3.6 percent; Reykjavik Free Church, 2.9 percent; Hafnarfjorour Free Church, 2 percent; The Independent Congregation, 1 percent; other religions, 3.9 percent (includes Pentecostal and Asatru Association); none, 5.6 percent; other or unspecified, 7.2 percent (2015)

BIRTH RATE
13.91 births/1,000 Icelanders (2015)

DEATH RATE
6.28 deaths/1,000 Icelanders (2015)

LIFE EXPECTANCY AT BIRTH
Total: 82.97 years
Male: 80.81 years
Female: 85.22 years (2015)

MAIN LANGUAGES
Icelandic, English, Nordic languages, German widely spoken

NATIONAL HOLIDAYS
New Year's Day (January 1), Maundy Thursday (on the Thursday before Easter), Good Friday (on the Friday before Easter), Easter Sunday, Easter Monday, First Day of Summer (third or fourth Thursday in April), May Day (May 1), Ascension Day (sixth Thursday after Easter), Whit Sunday (eighth Monday after Easter), Independence Day (June 17), Commerce Day (first Monday of August), Christmas Day (December 25), Boxing Day (December 26)

TIMELINE

IN ICELAND	IN THE WORLD
	323 BCE Alexander the Great's empire stretches from Greece to India.
	600 CE Height of Mayan civilization.
700 CE Irish monks arrive in Iceland.	
874 Norse settlers arrive. The Saga Age begins.	
930 The Icelandic Althing is founded.	
1000 Christianity becomes official religion.	**1000** The Chinese perfect gunpowder and begin to use it in warfare.
	1100 Rise of the Incan Civilization in Peru.
1220–1262 The Sturlunga Age: a period of anarchy	**1206** Genghis Khan unifies the Mongols and starts conquest of the world.
1262 Iceland is ruled by the king of Norway.	
1380 Iceland and Norway enter a union with Denmark.	**1558–1603** Reign of Elizabeth I of England
	1776 US Declaration of Independence
1783–1784 Laki volcanic eruption devastates Iceland.	**1789–1799** The French Revolution
1800 The Danish king abolishes the Althing; Icelanders begin to seek independence.	**1800** The start of the Industrial Age
	1861 The US Civil War begins.
	1869 The Suez Canal opens.
1904 Iceland is granted home rule.	**1914** World War I begins.
1915 Iceland gets its own flag.	
	1939 World War II begins.
1944 Iceland becomes an independent republic.	

IN ICELAND	IN THE WORLD
	1945
1949	The United States drops atomic bombs on
Iceland becomes a founding member of	Hiroshima and Nagasaki.
NATO.	
1951	
The United States builds the Keflavík	**1957**
airbase.	Russia launches *Sputnik*.
	1966–1969
	The Chinese Cultural Revolution.
1980	
Vigdís Finnbogadottir becomes first woman	
democratically elected as head of state.	
1986	**1986**
Presidents Gorbachev and Reagan meet at	Nuclear power disaster at Chernobyl in Ukraine
Reykjavik to discuss ending the Cold War.	**1991**
1994	Breakup of the Soviet Union
Iceland enters the European Economic	**1997**
Area.	Britain returns Hong Kong to China.
2000	
Reykjavik is voted the European City of	**2001**
Culture for the millennium.	Terrorists crash planes in New York,
	Washington, DC, and Pennsylvania.
	2003
	War in Iraq begins.
2008	**2008**
Three major Icelandic banks fail in the	United States elects first African American
midst of global economic downturn.	president, Barack Obama.
2010	
The Eyjafjallajokull volcano erupts; ash	
disrupts flights throughout Europe for months.	
2012	
President Olafur Ragnar Grimsson wins a	
record fifth term in office.	**2015–2016**
2016	ISIS launches terror attacks in France and
Prime Minister Sigmundur Gunnlaugsson	Belgium.
steps down after being implicated in the	
"Panama Papers." Sigurdur Ingi Johannsson	
becomes interim prime minister.	
Gudni Johannesson is elected president.	

GLOSSARY

Althing
The Icelandic parliament, founded in CE 930 and still functioning.

berserkir (BAIR-zerh-kahr)
Medieval warriors who dedicated themselves to Odin.

brennivín (BREN-i-vin)
A type of vodka made from distilled potatoes and flavored with angelica.

geyser
A hot-water spring that builds up pressure so that it shoots a jet of water high into the air.

glíma (GLEE-mah)
A traditional form of wrestling in which wrestlers wear harnesses on their thighs and hips which their opponent grabs in an attempt to throw them to the ground.

godi; pl. *godar* (GO-thi; GO-thar)
The chieftains of medieval Iceland.

hákarl (HAO-kahl)
Shark meat that has been matured by burying it for three to six months to allow it to putrefy. It is eaten raw in small chunks.

hangikjöt (HANG-i-YOHT)
Literally hung-lamb; a dish made of lamb that has been hung to be smoke-cured.

patronymic
The system of identifying someone by using their father's name followed by the Icelandic term for -son or -daughter.

Ragnarok
Doom of the gods; the final battle when the gods of Norse pagan tradition will lose to the forces that oppose them.

saltkjöt (SALT-kyoht)
Salt-mutton; a way of preserving lamb.

sandur (SAND-or)
Wastelands of black sand and volcanic debris deposited by run-off flowing from glaciers.

skalds (SKAHLDS)
The poets who recited Old Icelandic poetry.

skyr (SKOOR)
A yogurt-like dairy product made from milk curd.

slátur (SLAO-tor)
Offal from a sheep minced together with its blood and served in the sheep's stomach.

solfataras
Areas of hot ground associated with volcanic activity.

thing (thing)
A local parliament and meeting place in the Middle Ages.

FOR FURTHER INFORMATION

BOOKS

Bain, Carolyn, and Alexis Averbuck. *Lonely Planet Iceland*. New York: Lonely Planet, 2015.

DK. *Top 10 Iceland*. New York: DK Publishing, 2016.

Gíslason, Gunnar Karl, and Jody Eddy. *North: The New Nordic Cuisine of Iceland*. Berkeley, CA: Ten Speed Press, 2014.

Kellogg, Robert, and Jane Smiley. *The Sagas of Icelanders*. New York: Penguin Books, 2001.

ONLINE

BBC News Iceland country profile. www.bbc.com/news/world-europe-17383525

CIA World Factbook. Iceland. https://www.cia.gov/library/publications/the-world-factbook/geos/ic.html

Iceland Review. icelandreview.com

The Reykjavik Grapevine. grapevine.is

The Official Gateway to Iceland. www.iceland.is

BIBLIOGRAPHY

BBC News Iceland country profile. www.bbc.com/news/world-europe-17383525.

CIA World Factbook. Iceland. https://www.cia.gov/library/publications/the-world-factbook/geos/ic.html.

Eysteinsson, Thröstur. "Forestry in a treeless land." Iceland Forest Service, 2013. http://www.skogur.is/media/ymislegt/Treeless-land_netutgafa.pdf.

Fjörukráin. Viking Festival 2016. http://fjorukrain.is/en.

Iceland Monitor. http://icelandmonitor.mbl.is.

International Organization for Migration. http://www.iom.int/world-migration.

Kaplan, Sarah. "Climate change, melting glaciers make Iceland spring upward like a trampoline." *The Washington Post*, February 2, 2015. https://www.washingtonpost.com/news/morning-mix/wp/2015/02/02/climate-change-melting-glaciers-make-iceland-spring-upward-like-a-trampoline.

Katz, Cheryl. "Iceland's Vanishing Ice." *The Daily Climate*, December 18, 2013. http://www.dailyclimate.org/tdc-newsroom/2013/12/iceland-ice-climate.

Lovgren, Stefan. "'Sagas' Portray Iceland's Viking History." *National Geographic News*. May 7, 2004. http://news.nationalgeographic.com/news/2004/05/0507_040507_icelandsagas.html.

Lynskey, Joe. "Iceland: How a country with 329,000 people reached Euro 2016." *BBC Sport*. November 15, 2015. http://www.bbc.com/sport/football/30012357.

Prime Minister's Office. https://eng.forsaetisraduneyti.is.

Saga Museum. http://www.sagamuseum.is.

Statistics Iceland. "Iceland in Figures 2016." https://hagstofa.is/media/49863/icelandinfigures2016.pdf.

INDEX

INDEX